# EYES TO SEE
# AND EARS
# TO HEAR

# EYES TO SEE AND EARS TO HEAR

## WHAT JESUS REALLY MEANT

JOSEPH A.
TALAMO, PH.D.

gatekeeper press
Where Authors are Family
Tampla, Florida

Eyes to See and Ears to Hear: What Jesus Really Meant

Published by Gatekeeper Press
7853 Gunn Hwy., Suite 209
Tampa, FL 33626
www.GatekeeperPress.com

Library of Congress Control Number: 2023921072

ISBN (hardcover): 9781662945465
ISBN (paperback): 9781662945472
eISBN: 9781662945489

You told me to show you something worth seeing.
I show you yourself.

(Ged – The Tombs of Atuan)[1]

**Dedication**

Jesus and Buddha

Family, Friends, APM

C.G. Jung (1875-1961), M.D.

M-L. Von Franz (1915-1998), Ph.D.

E.F. Edinger (1922-1998), M.D.

The Dragonborn (1999-present)

---

1.    from U. LeGuin – The Tombs of Atuan

# Contents

# Introduction and Summary of Jungian-Based Psychology

This is a book for those with eyes to see and ears to hear, and to help those who do not yet have these to develop them. Anyone immersed in any organized religion or who has a closed mind should perhaps tread very carefully here. This is a situation of red pill/blue pill straight out of the blockbuster movie series *The Matrix*. Most people go through life in a relatively unaware and unchallenged state, unconsciously being fed the blue pill. There really isn't even a choice. There are also many for whom the blue pill is the appropriate one to take (absolutely no judgment intended). A few foolishly take the red pill without any idea what they are actually doing, and some unfortunate people end up effectively taking the red pill without much say in the matter. The red pill brings greater conscious awareness, but adds a burden that relatively few can yet comprehend. There are, of course, mixed states and even states where both are taken (often with cases of psychological disturbances). But then there is a generally small group of people who are actually presented with a true choice. When this happens, there is usually no option in reality but to take the red pill and everything that comes with it, though the pressure to take the blue pill is often great because it is the path of least resistance. Getting the red pill is like opening Pandora's box, but sometimes such things must be done for the sake of consciousness, development, and transformation. These are the people for whom this book is most written.

I do not expect any believing Christian to pursue these thoughts of mine any further, for they will probably seem to him absurd. I am not, however, addressing myself to the happy possessors of faith, but to those many people for whom the light has gone out, the mystery has faded, and God is dead. For most of them there is no going back, and one does not know either whether going back is always the better way. To gain an understanding of religious matters, probably all that is left us today is the psychological approach. (C.G. Jung)[2]

Anyone who thinks God should be discarded, does not exist, or holds other such views should also beware. Both groups are significantly out of touch with reality. This does not imply inferiority in any way; rather, the evolution that is likely to affect an increasing number of people has not yet hit for a variety of reasons. What Jesus really meant has to be received by an observer in the proper state, a fundamental feature of quantum physics and Jungian-based psychology. These are the only current guides we have in this quest. No judgment is ever intended in this book regarding people, only ideas and actions. Not everything is for everyone, but it needs to become for everyone sooner rather than later. People have to know the *whole* truth. It isn't a matter of *right and wrong*, but an issue of *complete and incomplete.*

The clergy usually are trapped by the dogmas of their religious systems, and unfortunately many have become the modern day

---

2.    C.G. Jung – Psychology and Religion [CW 11, para. 148, p. 89]; A. Ulanov mentions in Finding Space that depth psychology is necessary for religion to be meaningful and survive today.

Pharisees and Sadducees. They may mean well, but their input is often contrary to what Jesus and others were trying to convey. And they preach half-truths far too often.

> Until recently, the eternal images of the soul have been contained in the prevailing symbol-systems of organized religion. As traditional religion lost its capacity to carry living meaning, society was left without a containing vessel for transpersonal symbols. (E.F. Edinger)[3]

Then you have the overly peaceful people who will not stand for what is right in a given context, and so they fall for anything. They are somewhat like Essenes. And you have the overly militant and often incorrect people who try to take down everything that really matters in many areas. Their blindness reminds one of the Zealots. These things are shrouded in mystery to prevent those not yet ready from knowing them. That is why Jesus spoke in riddles and contradictions so often. It is also because different contexts call for different approaches. But all contexts call for the courage to speak truth and act on it. I am certain beyond any doubt that if Jesus were here today, there would not be a pew left standing in any church, much like the tables in the Temple episode that we will see.

Today, the Church and Jesus are not exactly linked anymore in any meaningful way, as the locus of connection is shifting from external to internal. The call is not for the abolition of organized religion, but rather its evolution. Theologians and traditional religious writers of any system or denomination end up making

---

3.    from E.F. Edinger – Melville's Moby Dick: An American Nekiya (p. 12)

circular arguments, playing mind games, and, in effect, end up trying to "know" an area that is quantum in nature via Newtonian methods and analysis, to borrow a physics analogy. An inappropriate approach leads to skewed conclusions that ultimately lead us away from the whole truth that sets us free.

The Grail Legend shows this observer effect well; the hero Perceval cannot even see the Grail until he is in the right (psychological) state to do so[4]. Jesus knew the danger of the Tree of Knowledge in the wrong hands. But one must go through it to reach the Tree of Life as some versions of the story illustrate[5]. Likewise, in Greek Mythology, Prometheus had to steal the fire from the gods, an equivalent action but without the judgment tone found in Christianity[6]. This is the *individuation* process by which we develop and transform. By going through this process and examining what Jesus really meant, we get ourselves, others, and the universe to a more complete state. The time has come to unlock these insights and put them into action. Closed eyes and ears are no longer an option as we now have the means to understand.

When the early Church was forming, all competition had to be removed for it to survive[7]. But the law of conservation of energy and matter says this cannot happen. What is repressed

---

4.   E. Jung & M-L. von Franz – The Grail Legend; the observer affecting the observed at the quantum level was proven by the famous double-slit experiments – see Hawking & Mlodinow: The Grand Design.
5.   E.F. Edinger - Ego and Archetype
6.   E.F. Edinger – The Eternal Drama: The Inner Meaning of Greek Mythology
7.   E.F. Edinger - The Psyche in Antiquity - Book II: Early Christianity and Gnosticism

or suppressed will go into the unconscious, take on a life of its own, and re-emerge under the right conditions. This is what happened with Gnosticism, alchemy, and other "heresies," and even the Gospel of Thomas, which was in the original canon but removed. Therefore, much of what Jesus said is *not* included in the current Gospels. Apocryphal texts are very critical. So we will of course look everywhere necessary for the truth, implicitly and/or explicitly. Jung did this especially with Gnosticism and even more so with alchemy. Furthermore, in antiquity, everything was literal and concrete, because that is where people were. That is not where we are today, whether we know it or not.

Until the early 1900s, when giants such as Swiss psychiatrist C.G. Jung (1875-1961) and quantum physicist Wolfgang Pauli (1900-1958) came along, as well as Niels Bohr (complementarity[8]), Max Planck, and others, we did not have the awareness to make sense of this material. The German philosopher Immanuel Kant knew things earlier, but not psychologically, as the human psyche was not yet evolved enough to understand. *Psychology in its true form and spirituality cannot be separated.*

In 1912, Jung wrote *Symbols of Transformation*, breaking with Freud and giving us the ability to understand. But not until the 1950s was this complete. *Aion, Answer to Job*, and *Mysterium Coniunctionis* were written by Jung, his three most significant works, between 1951 and 1956. During his confrontation with the unconscious, covering roughly 1912-1928, Jung wrote and

---

8.   This works psychologically as well – see M-L Von Franz – C.G. Jung: His Myth in Our Time

drew the Red Book, which recently was released to the public in 2009. All of these books are difficult, but we will hit them all as they largely hold the keys we need, especially in the Gospel of John. That means humanity has had about 65-70 years to even be exposed to this material, not nearly enough for the changes we need to take root. There has not been enough time to build the *critical mass* of people to understand and implement the material. This book aims to help this process along and help navigate the current transitional, or *apocalyptic*, period we are in now[9].

The first Gospel to be written was Mark in about 60 A.D. Matthew and Luke followed in the 70 A.D. range. John was written around 90-100 A.D. and is different from the three synoptic Gospels. They all were written well after Jesus' lifetime, which ended in actuality around 29 A.D., not 33 A.D. as commonly believed. He was probably born around 4 B.C. The point is the evangelists would not have written about Jesus during or near his life, which makes things a bit difficult. But the message is consistent, lending credence to the material. It is found in all spiritual and mythological systems as well. *But often the meaning, not the literality, is the key.*

Analysis will be done as we go through each Gospel, but three concepts are needed now. They will make more sense later, but they need to be established here. The first is the *ego*, which is the center of the consciously aware personality. The second is the *Self*, which is the totality and center of the psyche, the God-image, and transcends space and time. It is the central *archetype*, the third concept, which is an autonomous entity existing outside of space-

9.    E.F. Edinger – Archetype of the Apocalypse

time but which may incarnate in any number of ways. These are universal principles found in all times and cultures, even those never contacting each other. Examples include the hero, mother, father, wounded healer, God, and many more. The combination and transcendence of all Selves is the Cosmic Self, which is what people call God[10]. The connection between the ego and the Self is called the ego-Self axis, and it is living and bidirectional. An archetype exists *a priori*, meaning we do not create it[11].

In itself, an archetype is neither good nor evil. It is morally neutral, like the gods of antiquity, and becomes good or evil only by contact with the conscious mind, or else a paradoxical mixture of both. Whether it will be conducive to good or evil is determined, knowingly or unknowingly, by the conscious attitude. (C.G. Jung)[12]

The most accurate metaphor I know for God and the universe is the Force in *Star Wars*, but no human can fully know God. It is like a limit or other asymptotic function in calculus or Plato's allegory of the cave. We pick up bits and pieces and must piece together the puzzle as best we can. Like the Force in *Star Wars*, God is in everything, including each of us, and there are two sides in each case, a light and a dark. Jesus will say this, as we will see, but not obviously so. We have to interpret it via Jungian-based

---

10.  E.F. Edinger – Ego and Self: The Old Testament Prophets; in Jungian-based psychology, one will encounter the terms God and God-image. This is a complex subject, but in short, God means God and the God-image is God for each individual or group.

11.  This paragraph is pulled from many sources; e.g. C.G. Jung – Archetypes of the Collective Unconscious (CW 9(i)) and E.F. Edinger – Science of the Soul: A Jungian Perspective.

12.  from C.G. Jung – Psychology and Literature [CW 15, para. 160, p. 104]

psychology and quantum physics. However, the point is made directly in the Yin-Yang, which clearly demonstrates the reality of the union of opposites in *Tao*. The Hindu analog is *Atman*. There will be much more on these topics to come, but for now, know that reality, including God, is generally not either/or, but both/and, just like we are. Humans are made in the image and likeness of God, from which we can infer that God is also dual[13].

This is perhaps the greatest thing about Job, that, faced with this difficulty, he does not doubt the unity of God. He clearly sees that God is at odds with himself – so totally at odds that he, Job, is quite certain of finding in God a helper and an "advocate" against God. As certain as he is of the evil in Yahweh, he is equally certain of the good.

(C.G. Jung)[14]

Christ, as a hero and god-man, signifies psychologically the self; that is, he represents the projection of this most important and most central of archetypes. The archetype of the self has, functionally, the significance of a ruler of the inner world, i.e., of the collective unconscious. The self, as a symbol of wholeness, is a *coincidentia oppositorum*, and therefore contains light and darkness simultaneously. In the Christ-figure the opposites which are united in the archetype

13.  Richard Rohr interprets the terms image and likeness in his daily meditations via CAC differently, but I see no reason to add interpretation to a clearly established Biblical concept. This is in keeping with the philosophical principle of Occam's Razor, which states that the *simplest yet accurate* explanation is the best.
14.  C.G. Jung – Answer to Job [CW 11, para. 567, p. 369]; Meister Eckhart had a prayer expressly asking God for help against God (see J. Dourley – On Behalf of the Mystical Fool: Jung on the Religious Situation).

are polarized into the "light" son of God on the one hand and the devil on the other. The original unity of opposites is still discernible in the original unity of Satan and Yahweh.

(C.G. Jung)[15]

What Jesus was talking about is often archetypal in nature, and we would hear similar statements from others, like Buddha. Each one is an incarnation of the Self. There have been many, and there will be more to come, though not necessarily in the form of an outward figure. This is because of an era shift, an apocalyptic moment, that we are now experiencing from a spiritual perspective. Jesus will speak of this in Matthew, so we will discuss that when we get there. The point now is that Jesus cannot be the be all and end all when, for example, both Osiris and the phoenix, both out of Egyptian mythology and coming before Him, are incarnations of the exact same archetype, that of death and rebirth (of the god). Each of us goes through this as we carry our crosses as well. In addition, the Christian Trinity is derived from the Egyptian trinity, which consists of God the father, Pharoah the son, and *ka*, which is the life force or spirit[16].

Between the opposites there arises spontaneously a symbol of unity and wholeness, no matter whether it reaches consciousness or not. Should something extraordinary or impressive then occur in the outside world, be it a human personality, a thing, or an idea, the unconscious content can project itself upon it, thereby investing the projection carrier with numinous and mythical powers. Thanks to its

---

15.   C.G. Jung – Symbols of Transformation [CW 5, para. 576, p. 368]
16.   see E.F. Edinger – The Mysterium Lectures

numinosity, the projection carrier has a highly suggestive effect and grows into a saviour myth whose basic features have been repeated countless times. (C.G. Jung)[17]

But from the Christian perspective, Jesus is the primary figure, though today in the form of the Holy Spirit. The astrological shift in 2000 A.D. from Pisces, the fish, a well-known symbol of Jesus, to Aquarius, the water bearer, illustrates this point. We must now largely carry our own water psychologically, and salvation lies within for the most part. Conscious awareness and direct experience of the archetypal/divine (to the extent possible) are the keys[18]. This is why Adam and Eve *had* to eat the apple, and why Prometheus stole fire from the gods in the Greek tradition[19]. There would be no human or divine development without it. And let's not forget:

They were perfect creatures of God, for He created only perfection, and yet they committed the first sin....How was that possible? They could not have done it if God had not placed in them the possibility of doing it. That was clear, too, from the serpent, whom God had created before them, obviously so that it could induce Adam and Eve to sin....
*Therefore it was God's intention that they should sin.*
(C.G. Jung)[20]

Great saints were, as we know, sometimes great heretics, so it is probable that anyone who has immediate experience of God is a little bit outside the organization one calls the Church. The

---

17.   C.G Jung – Civilization in Transition [CW 10, para. 784, p. 414-415]
18.   E.F. Edinger – The Creation of Consciousness and quantum physics
19.   see E.F. Edinger – The Eternal Drama: The Inner Meaning of Greek Mythology
20.   as cited in M-L Von Franz - C.G. Jung: His Myth in Our Time, p. 159

Church itself would have been in a pretty pass if the Son of God had remained a law-abiding Pharisee, a point one tends to forget. (C.G. Jung)[21]

The final area to discuss before delving into the Gospels is the question of whether or not God exists. Jung and Pauli worked somewhat jointly on a concept called *synchronicity*[22]. So many people have had these types of experiences arising out of the non-space-time bound realm of the collective unconscious (i.e. the divine), where the archetypes exist, that they cannot be ignored. Here are some examples:

> For example, a patient, whose problem lay in her excessive and seemingly intractable rationalism, was telling Jung about an impressive dream in which she had been given a costly jewel in the form of a scarab beetle. Just at that moment an insect began tapping against the consulting room window. Jung let it in, caught it in his hands and, realizing it was a form of scarabaeid beetle, presented it to his patient with the words, 'Here is your scarab'. The irrationality yet obvious meaningfulness of this paralleling between real life and her dream was so striking that it broke through the patient's resistances and enabled her treatment to proceed[23].

Jung cites as an illustration Emanuel Swedenborg's well-attested vision of the great fire in Stockholm in 1759. Swedenborg was at a party in Gottenburg about 200 miles

21.  C.G. Jung – Psychology and Religion [CW 11, para. 481, p. 321]
22.  C.G. Jung – Dream Symbols of the Individuation Process and Synchronicity: An Acausal Connecting Principle (CW 8)
23.  from R. Main – Encountering Jung: Jung on Synchronicity and the Paranormal, p. 8-9

from Stockholm when the vision occurred. He told his companions at six o'clock in the evening that the fire had started, then described its course over the next two hours, exclaiming in relief at eight o'clock that it had at last been extinguished, just three doors from his own house. All these details were confirmed when messengers arrived in Gottenburg from Stockholm over the next few days[24].

An example mentioned by Jung is of a student friend of his whose father had promised him a trip to Spain if he passed his final examinations satisfactorily. The friend then had a dream of seeing various things in a Spanish city: a particular square, a Gothic Cathedral and, around a certain corner, a carriage drawn by two cream-coloured horses. Shortly afterwards, having successfully passed his examinations, he actually visited Spain for the first time and encountered all the details from his dream in reality [25].

In the first example, which is a classic case of synchronicity, the patient was able to get through her impasse in treatment via the presence of the scarab beetle appearing at the therapy room window (physical event) *and* in her dream (psychological event). Obviously, the connection between the actual scarab appearing and the presence of the scarab in her dream was not based on cause and effect in the standard, space-time sense.

---

24. from R. Main – Encountering Jung: Jung on Synchronicity and the Paranormal, p. 20-21
25. from R. Main – Encountering Jung: Jung on Synchronicity and the Paranormal, p. 21

Recall what we said earlier about universal principles, or archetypes, and how they operate outside of space-time boundaries. If we turn to Egyptian mythology, we find that a scarab beetle is actually a symbol of the archetype of *rebirth*, which is precisely what the patient needed, psychologically speaking, in her life at this time. To understand what transpired here, we must realize that there is an archetype (rebirth) behind the whole process. The actual scarab and the dream scarab are both space-time manifestations of a psychological process (rebirth) operating not entirely within space and time.

The other two examples about the Stockholm fire and the Spanish city represent, respectively, a relativization of space and a relativization of time. Swedenborg was able to describe the course of the fire in real time even though he was not in the same space as it was taking place, and the student was able to perceive the nature of the space in question (Spanish city) even though the time of the visit and the experience of things in the Spanish city were not the same (he had not yet been there).

There are enough instances of people experiencing these synchronistic events, along with the repeated confirmation of the *nonlocality* concept in quantum physics, that we cannot dismiss them as unreal or illegitimate. *In quantum physics, synchronicity is known as nonlocality, and both prove beyond any reasonable doubt, if not outright, the existence of God*[26]. But we have to evaluate in terms of meaning, not cause and effect, because we are dealing

---

26.  The danger of atheism, in addition to not being supported by the data, is that such an individual may be at risk of substituting himself/herself for God, never a wise move.

with entities not entirely within space-time. In addition to *why*, we must learn to ask *what for*. The rules are not the same, and the data is not of the same nature as in our space-time everyday world. However, both sets of rules simultaneously exist and interact with each other, so how do we reconcile this fact?

Thankfully, we have *symbols*, which are transformers of energy between the archetypal, non-space-time realm and our everyday space-time bound world, such as the cross, the phoenix, the Yin-Yang, and many others, to guide us. For those with knowledge of the science in quantum physics, there will be no collapsing of the wave function to zero, as happens in our macro, space-time bound world. These archetypal energies have no substance in the common sense of the word, and so they are quantum in nature.

Ultimately, the path to God is through our personal suffering, which is rooted in the archetypal psyche, and our ability to transform it.

Through the perfection of victory they achieve health, but the soul enters through the hole of defeat. (Robert Bly)[27]

We should not try to "get rid" of a neurosis, but rather to experience what it means, what it has to teach, what its purpose is. We should even learn to be thankful for it, otherwise we pass it by and miss the opportunity of getting to know ourselves as we really are. A neurosis is truly removed only when it has removed the false attitude of the ego. We do not cure it – it cures us. A man is ill, but the illness is nature's attempt to heal him. From the illness itself we can learn so

---

27.   from Robert Bly – Iron John, p. 210

much for our recovery, and what the neurotic flings away as
absolutely worthless contains the true gold we should never
have found elsewhere.

(C.G. Jung)[28]

This means we have to take an honest look at our *shadow*, or
undeveloped, areas, and our *complexes*, which involve unhealthy,
often predictable, behaviors in a given context. Complexes will
have an archetypal core, which makes them very powerful and
gripping[29]. For example, many mother complexes may involve
Aphrodite or Artemis, even though these are only archetypal
images, not the archetypes themselves. Effectively, you would
be dealing with both the personal mother and the archetypal
mother here. Anyone who has experienced difficulty separating
from a jealous mother (Aphrodite with her son Eros/Cupid)
or a mother without boundaries (Artemis with Actaeon),
respectively, knows this, at least in the unconscious. The same
goes for those still living in fear of their fathers in context of
Zeus (detached) or Yahweh (overly involved). One must be able
to identify the core to make any progress that lasts. Mythology,
fairy tales, and dreams contain much information pertaining
to these archetypal areas, and the data is the same, though in
different forms, across all times and places.

Jungian-based psychology is all about identity, meaning,
development, and transformation. *Alchemy* is a brilliant

---

28.   from C.G. Jung - The State of Psychotherapy Today, [CW 10, para. 361,
       p. 170]
29.   E.F. Edinger – Science of the Soul: A Jungian Perspective; complexes
       also isolate people from the whole, as C.G. Jung notes in his ETH
       Lectures from 1934 (Consciousness and the Unconscious).

metaphor for these processes; it was never really about making gold, though that is what the alchemists thought. Rather, it is all about the above Jungian areas, especially the realization of the Self in the form of the Philosopher's Stone[30]. We often start with the black, or *nigredo*, the darkness that grips our psyches. Then we go through the whiteness, or *albedo*, which brings superficial awareness or light to us. Next comes red, or *rubedo*, which means now we have entered the real, "bloody" reality we call development and transformation. Finally, we get the aforementioned gold or yellow, which is the goal of completeness at a new level regarding the Self[31]. Jung's most elaborate and developed imagery of the Self comes from Ezekiel's grand vision in the Old Testament and is discussed at length by Edinger in both *The Aion Lectures* and *The Mysterium Lectures*. This is way beyond the scope of our discussion here.

The Axiom of Maria Prophetissa in alchemy illustrates such processes. *One becomes two, two becomes three, and out of the third comes the fourth which is One.* Yahweh becomes Jesus, Jesus becomes the Holy Spirit, and then, as the Eastern faiths do, if you add evil or, alternatively but certainly not equivalently, add

---

30.  C.G. Jung – Psychology and Alchemy (CW 12); M-L. Von Franz – Alchemy; E.F. Edinger – Anatomy of the Psyche

31.  E.F. Edinger - The Mysterium Lectures; in Dream Symbols of the Individuation Process, C.G. Jung notes the four colors of the four functions: Thinking (blue), Intuition (yellow), Sensation (green), and Feeling (red). The goal is to progress through all four functions (there are actually eight when introversion and extraversion are combined with the four core types – see M-L Von Franz, Psychotherapy, for a detailed discussion of all eight types) and transcend them all at a new level of consciousness and transformation.

the feminine, which has effectively been done with the light side in Mary[32], you now have the completed *quaternio* (four) which is One[33]. And that is exactly how it works in Christianity. Jesus will show this in the Gospels, especially John. Thomas Aquinas, to whom Aurora Consurgens[34] is attributed, refers to alchemy as a "sacrament," and notes that it has the power to transform and heal just as God does. This is having eyes to see and ears to hear.

*Karma* is a well-known concept from the East that states the universe[35] (God) will show you the face you show it and the entities comprising it. This is synchronistic in nature and, trust me, very real. To avoid negative effects, the proper *conscious attitude* must be present, meaning ultimately to face yourself and reality as they are, no matter the cost. Our future as a race depends on it, as does that of the universe from a psychological standpoint.

To help with this, we have to develop a much higher level of courage, but we also need to understand ourselves. *Active*

32. Sophia accomplishes the addition of the light and dark sides of the feminine as the female consort of Yahweh, though this is hidden by the organized forms of the faith, and she may be found in the book of Wisdom, which is the meaning of her name.
33. Adding the body to the spiritual Trinity also creates a necessary and more complete quaternity.
34. see M-L. Von Franz: Aurora Consurgens, a companion volume to Mysterium Coniunctionis, where she lays this out. No one is absolutely certain who wrote the piece since the original has been lost, but the meaning of the recorded visions and experiences remains the same and points to what we have just mentioned.
35. The multiverse theory (M Theory) doesn't change anything we are saying here. See Hawking & Mlodinow: The Grand Design. In fact, there are parallels between this and the many Selves combing to form the Cosmic Self. See J. Talamo: M Theory and the Cosmic Self (unpublished).

*imagination* is an exercise by which we can dialogue with the images in our psyches. It is like consciously tapping into the dream world while awake. This is not psychotic in any way, but a conversation between ego and Self[36]. Also necessary is *amplification*, which is linking psychological material to archetypal data arising out of dreams, myths, and fairy tales, among other areas. This is important because these are the three primary ways in which material from the archetypal realm (God's realm) reaches us.

Let's now see how Jesus makes all of this clear[37]. Any time we hear something like "whoever has ears to hear ought to hear" or Amen, I say to you," we need to pay special attention. Straight healing episodes may be treated as repeats because the meaning is the same: the Self is the guide to healing and transformation. The type of malady doesn't change this universal fact, though it is especially true with psychological conditions, which are our real final frontier as humans. When Jesus expels demons, he is almost certainly curing psychological issues (the only type never named as what they are), as people tended to attribute to negative divine forces that which they could not understand. Finally, we must pay attention to what Jesus does *not* say in context of what he says. So many things are present by their absence, and there are many elephants in the room, as it were.

---

36. Active Imagination is contraindicated for people with latent or expressed psychoses, as well as a few others, in many cases. For a more complete discussion, see M-L. Von Franz – Psychotherapy.
37. All Bible quotes from The Living Bible (with a few from the Catholic Study Bible).

This entire endeavor is worth it because Jesus is such an important figure regardless of spiritual background. Without a both/and attitude instead of an either/or one, we won't be able to get the message, at times even when it appears Jesus is being black and white. People of that time, and even today, could not think any other way, so he had to speak as if things that are not really split are. Jesus also will say one thing at one time and the opposite thing at another time, and that is because reality is based on the opposites and context always matters. *Ambiguity and paradox are key.* This will become clear by the end of the book.

The way I would suggest reading this book, which includes every word Jesus said in the Gospels and a few comments from elsewhere, is for the reader to make sure he/she has a solid grasp of the Introduction just presented before proceeding. Then, take a few passages and let them digest for a bit before moving forward. The writing style is direct and dense, so it can be profitable to approach the material in this way, allowing your psyche to interact with it and see what emerges.

## Mark (Symbol: Lion)

Mark's Gospel was the first to be written and is also the shortest of the four. It is pretty bare bones overall while concisely covering the major aspects of Jesus' story.

Mark 1:15 At last the time has come. God's Kingdom is near! Turn from your sins and act on this glorious news!

Here we have the demand from the Self to become more connected to it; in other words, to strengthen the ego-Self axis. Sin is a state of being disconnected from the Self (God-image) and can obviously come about in various ways. Anything that does not foster identity, meaning, development, and transformation may be viewed as sinful, regardless of if we are referring to an act of commission or omission. Hard as this often is, individuation is the goal towards which we must all strive.

Mark 1:17 Come, follow me! **And I will make you fishermen for the souls of men**.

Jesus, being a symbol of the Self for Christians, shows here that following and acting on the demands of the Self will not only transform you, but allow you to bring others along as well. This is how things develop and evolve.

Mark 1:34 But he refused to allow the demons to speak, because they knew who he was.

Our demons, who take advantage of our undeveloped shadow areas and complexes, always know who we are. But Jesus, being individuated to the degree that he was, had the ability to keep demons at bay. That is the power of consciousness, development, and transformation.

Mark 1:38 We must go to other towns as well, and give my message to them too, for that is why I came.

The divine message is indeed meant for everyone, and it arrives via manifestations of the Self. For Christians, Jesus filled and continues to fill that role via the Holy Spirit.

Mark 1:41 I want to! Be healed!

The Self (symbolized for Christians by Jesus), is the source of healing and wholeness.

Mark 1:43-44 Go, and be examined immediately by the Jewish priest. Don't stop to speak to anyone along the way. Take along the offering prescribed by Moses for a leper who is healed, so that everyone will have proof that you are well again.

The idea here is that proper protocols are not abolished by archetypal intervention, but rather upheld, as Jesus will note about the Law. But there is no need to announce what has happened via the Self; one simply must live in accordance with the healing and transformation that has occurred.

Mark 2:5 Son, your sins are forgiven!

Connection to the Self in the proper way (correct conscious attitude) will result in freedom to move ahead.

Mark 2:8 Why does this bother you? I, the Messiah, have the authority to forgive sins. But talk is cheap-anyone could say that. So, I'll prove it to you by healing this man...Pick up your stretcher and go on home, for you are healed!

The Self always has the ultimate authority, and it backs up its messages with action, provided the recipient (ego) has the proper conscious attitude.

Mark 2:13 Come with me...Come be my disciple!

Jesus attempts to establish the ego-Self axis and unite human and divine.

Mark 2:17 Sick people need the doctor, not healthy ones! I haven't come to tell good people to repent, but the bad ones.

In reality, everyone has (psychological) work to do, but in some cases, development and transformation are blocked, often by stubborn complexes, to the point of triggering a response from the Self. There is more than the obvious reason for this, which we will discuss later. At any rate, it is ultimately foolish to ignore any contact arising from the Self.

Mark 2:19-22 Do friends of the bridegroom refuse to eat at the wedding feast? Should they be sad while he is with them? But some day he will be taken from them, and then they will mourn. [Besides, going without food is part of the old way of doing things.] It is like patching an old garment with unshrunk cloth. What happens? The patch pulls away and leaves the hole worse than before. **You know better than to put new wine into old wineskins. They would burst. The wine would be spilled out and the wineskins ruined. New wine needs fresh wineskins**.

Here we have a very important message from Jesus that goes way beyond simply trying to be in the moment, important as that may be. Jesus was generally not a fan of the old ways, though he understood them. Evolutions of any kind and increases in consciousness require updated containers to hold them. Everything, including conscious dominants and ideas, eventually wear out and must be refreshed. Jesus himself represents new wine compared to Yahweh, and the evolution from Yahweh to

Jesus is blatantly obvious if one spends even ten minutes apiece with the Old and New Testaments. This was also a critical theme regarding the old king in the Grail Legend mentioned earlier[38].

Mark 2:25-26 Didn't you ever hear about the time King David and his companions were hungry, and he went into the house of God-Abiathar was high priest then-and they ate the special bread only priests were allowed to eat? That was against the law too. But the Sabbath was made to benefit man, not man to benefit the Sabbath. And I, the Messiah, have authority even to decide what men can do on Sabbath days!

Again, Jesus isn't particularly keen on established customs; he's more interested in making things right and refreshing outdated material and ways.

Mark 3:4-5 Is it all right to do kind deeds on Sabbath days? Or is this a day for doing harm? Is it a day to save lives or destroy them?...Reach out your hand.

The exact point just mentioned.

Mark 3:23-29 How can Satan cast out Satan? A house divided against itself will collapse. A home filled with strife and division destroys itself. And if Satan is fighting against himself, how can he accomplish anything? He would never survive. [Satan must be bound before his demons can be cast out], just as a strong man must be tied up before his house can be robbed and his property ransacked. I solemnly declare that any sin of man can be forgiven, even blasphemy against me, but blasphemy against the Holy Spirit can never be forgiven. It is an eternal sin.

---

38.   see E. Jung & M-L. Von Franz – The Grail Legend

This is an absolutely critical passage found in other Gospels as well. We are all familiar with the notion of a divided body being unable to survive. Jesus left something out here, though as always he knew it. God is also fighting against God, as noted earlier and in material yet to come, and if Jesus was speaking to an Eastern audience instead of a Western one, the concept of two entities, God and Satan, would not even be mentioned. It would make no sense to a Hindu or Buddhist, for example, because in the East, God is explicitly acknowledged as a unity (Atman/Tao), and it's true everywhere; it just gets split by the more black/white thinking West. But Jesus knew it, and in John's Gospel, he will reveal the ingredient required to transcend the fight: a perceiving entity with sufficient consciousness.

The issue of the unforgivable sin, blasphemy against the Holy Spirit, makes sense because, from the Christian perspective, the Holy Spirit can be understood as the ultimate evolutionary form of God that unites and transcends all opposites and drives development and transformation towards completeness. When Yahweh refers to himself as I AM, the Holy Spirit fulfills that transformational aim. There is no "good" or "bad;" these are largely human constructs. The Holy Spirit, the Force in Star Wars, etc., are reality itself, and going against what IS in its most complete form cannot be excused. The same applies to failure to put *any* energy into development and transformation, even if we are all going to fall somewhat short.

Mark 3:35 Who is my mother? Who are my brothers?...These are my mother and brothers! Anyone who does God's will is my brother, and my sister, and my mother.

Anyone who is properly connected to the Self and is following its prescriptions is part of the Kingdom, as it were. It doesn't necessarily go by blood connection, but rather by conscious awareness and a healthy ego-Self axis.

Mark 4:3-9 Listen! A farmer decided to sow some grain. As he scattered it across his field, some of it fell on a path, and some birds came and picked it off the hard ground and ate it. Some fell on thin soil with underlying rock. It grew up quickly enough, but soon wilted beneath the hot sun and died because the roots had no nourishment in the shallow soil. Some seeds fell among thorns that shot up and crowded the young plants so that they produced no grain. But some seeds fell on good soil and yielded thirty times as much as he had planted – some of it even sixty or a hundred times as much. If you have ears, listen!

This is a vitally important message about receptivity to the requirements of the Self (the Word of God). We will address this in Matthew's Gospel in detail. It is the parable of the Sower.

Mark 4:11-25 **You are permitted to know some truths about the Kingdom of God that are hidden to those outside the Kingdom:** Though they see and hear, they will not turn to God, or be forgiven for their sins. But if you can't understand *this* simple illustration, what will you do about all the others I am going to tell? The farmer I talked about is anyone who brings God's message to others, trying to plant good seeds in their lives. The hard pathway, where some of the seed fell, represents the hard hearts of some of those who hear God's message; Satan comes at once to try to make them forget it. The rocky soil represents the hearts of those who hear the message with joy, but like young plants in such soil, their roots don't go very deep, and as soon as persecution begins, they wilt. The thorny ground represents the hearts of people who listen to the Good News and receive it, but all too quickly the attractions of this world and the delights of wealth, and the search for success and the lure of nice things come in, and crowd out God's message from their hearts, so that no crop is produced. But the good soil represents the hearts of those who truly hear God's message and produce a plentiful harvest for God-thirty, sixty, or even a hundred times as much as was planted in their hearts. Then He asked them, "When someone lights a lamp, does he put a box over it to shut out the light? Of course not! The light could not be seen or used. A lamp is placed on a stand to shine and be useful. All that is now hidden will someday come to light. If you have ears, listen! And be sure to put into practice what you hear. The more you do this, the more you will understand what I tell you. To him who has more shall be given; from him who has not shall be taken away even what he has.

Here we have an explanation of the parable of the Sower as well as a direct statement from Jesus himself that we *are* able, to a point, to be aware of God's nature. He also indicates that we are expected to get the messages coming from the Self; if he expected it of simple people two millennia ago, he certainly expects it of us today. We must use our light (consciousness) to understand such things, and nothing is concealed that will not be revealed by this light. And as always, Jesus has little tolerance for hypocrites who do not put insight into action. There is a potentially long period of endurance between insight and action according to Jung, however, and Jesus will note the same point in saying we will experience trouble in this world/mode of existence. If you have the eyes to see and ears to hear what the Self is communicating via consciousness awareness, more will indeed be given to you, but if your awareness/approach is lacking, even what you have will be lost. This is a hard truth, and if I'm being honest, I have work to do here. And you probably do as well.

Mark 4:26-29 Here is another story illustrating what the Kingdom of God is like: A farmer sowed his field, and went away, and as the days went by, the seeds grew and grew without his help. For the soil made the seeds grow. First a leaf blade pushed through, and later wheat heads formed and finally the grain ripened, and then the farmer came at once with his sickle and harvested it.

The Self sows the seeds of development and transformation in our psyches, provided our conscious attitudes are correct. Eventually, this will bear fruit, and we are "harvested" to a new level of awareness and being.

Mark 4:30-32 How can I describe the Kingdom of God? What story shall I use to illustrate it? It is like a mustard seed! Though this is one of the smallest of seeds, yet it grows to be among the largest of plants, with long branches where birds can build their nests and be sheltered.

The key idea here is that even the smallest amount of consciousness can be multiplied and help us grow into more complete people ready to experience the Kingdom. The only number that cannot multiply anything into at least something is zero; it always yields zero and stunts development and transformation.

Mark 4:33-40 Let's cross to the other side of the lake....Quiet down! (to the wind and sea)...Why were you so fearful? Don't you even yet have confidence in me?

Confidence in the direction provided by the Self is very important yet often hard to maintain. That's the main idea here.

Mark 5:7-9 Come out, you evil spirit...What is your name?

Naming things is crucial because it takes away their power. This is why saying "Voldemort" is preferred to "He-Who-Must-Not-Be Named" in *Harry Potter*, for example[39].

Mark 5:19 Go home to your friends, and tell them what wonderful things God has done for you, and how merciful he has been.

Talking about what one has experienced depends on the context. Here, Jesus is trying to show what the proper attitude towards the Self can do and how it needs to spread.

Mark 5:30-34 Who touched my clothes?...Daughter, your faith has made you well; go in peace, healed of your disease.

This is a major healing episode, and the idea is that healing requires contact with the Self and a belief that the proper conscious attitude in this regard will yield results, even if there are no guarantees.

Mark 5:36 Don't be afraid. Just trust me. Why all this weeping and commotion? The child isn't dead; she is only asleep! Get up, little girl! (referring to Jairus' daughter)

The healing of Jairus' daughter adds an additional point to the immediately preceding discussion. Jairus was not the type people

---

39.   see J.K. Rowling – Harry Potter (entire series).

would have expected Jesus to assist, but because he believed and had the proper connection with the Self, his daughter was cured.

Mark 6:4 **A prophet is recognized everywhere except in his hometown and among his relatives and by his own family.**

Even Jesus was rejected in his home area, and how often do our families and friends ignore advice that can be helpful because it comes from someone too close? It is unfortunately a frequent occurrence, and sometimes the message must be delivered by the "right" person to take effect.

Mark 6:10-11 Stay at one home in each village-don't shift around from house to house while you are there. **And whenever a village won't accept you or listen to you, shake the dust from your feet as you leave; it is a sign that you have abandoned it to its fate.**

This is a key passage with same point as the prophet/hometown issue, only with people not as close who refuse to pay attention. Sometimes, moving on (shaking the dust) is the only option. However, note that Jesus does not mention shaking the dust on anyone (taking revenge). Confucius said the same thing: "If you go on a journey of revenge, dig two graves." People are perfectly capable of burying themselves.

Mark 6:31-38 Let's get away for a while and rest....You feed them...How much food do we have? Go and find out (loaves and fishes).

Again, the Self will multiply and nourish with even the smallest amount of energy or resources. It just can't be zero.

Mark 6:50 It's all right...It is I! Don't be afraid. (Jesus walks on water)

Things that do not seem possible are possible with a healthy, living connection to the Self, which can effectively work miracles under these conditions.

Mark 7:6-13 You bunch of hypocrites! Isaiah the prophet described you very well when he said, 'These people speak very prettily about the Lord but they have no love for him at all. Their worship is a farce, for they claim God commands the people to follow their petty rules.' How right Isaiah was! For you ignore God's specific orders and substitute your own traditions. You are simply rejecting God's laws and trampling them under your feet for the sake of tradition. For instance, Moses gave you this law from God: Honor your father and mother. And he said anyone who speaks against his father or mother must die. But you say it is perfectly all right for a man to disregard his needy parents, telling them, Sorry, I can't help you! For I have given to God what I could have given to you. And so you break the law of God in order to protect your man-made traditions. And this is only one example. There are many, many others.

Again, Jesus is not a fan of hypocrites. Here, he rebukes the people in question for insisting upon ego-made rules instead of the much more complete Self-made rules. Actions will show true colors better than words.

Mark 7:14-16 All of you listen,...and try to understand. Your souls aren't harmed by what you eat, but by what you think and say!

Mark 7:18-23 Don't you understand either? Can't you see that what you eat won't harm your soul? For food doesn't come in contact with the heart, but only passes through the digestive system.

Mark 7:20-23 It is the thought that pollutes. For from within, out of men's hearts, come evil thoughts of lust, theft, murder, adultery, wanting what belongs to others, wickedness, deceit, lewdness, envy, slander, pride, and all other folly. All these vile things come from within; they are what pollute you and make you unfit for God.

These three short passages show that external rules and factors take a back seat to what is going on within.

Mark 7:27-29 First I should help my own family-the Jews. It isn't right to take the children's food and throw it to the dogs...Good! You have answered so well that I have healed your little girl. Go on home, for the demon has left her. (Syrophonecian woman's daughter)

Jesus is convinced to heal the woman's daughter, showing that our approach to the archetypal psyche affects its response to us. This mirroring effect is what lies behind the Eastern notion of karma. The Self does not discriminate in this regard; people of any type can be connected.

Mark 7:34 Open! (blind/deaf man)

Another healing episode with the same meaning attached.

Mark 8:1-5 I have pity for these people, for they have been here three days and have nothing left to eat. And if I send them home with nothing to eat, they will faint along the road! For some of them have come a long distance...How many loaves of bread do you have?

Same idea about multiplying our transformational efforts discussed above.

Mark 8:12 Certainly not. How many more miracles do you people need?

Even Jesus gets frustrated with the stubbornness of people, including the twelve apostles.

Mark 8:15-21 Beware of the yeast of King Herod and the Pharisees...No, that isn't it at all! Can't you understand? Are your hearts too hard to take it in? Your eyes are to see with-why don't you look? Why don't you open your ears and listen? Don't you remember anything at all? What about the 5,000 men I fed with five loaves of bread. How many basketfuls of scraps did you pick up afterwards? And when I fed the 4,000 with seven loaves, how much was left? And yet you think I'm worried that we have no bread?

This passage shows just how literal people of that time were. In our lives, external issues may appear to be responsible for our issues, and in certain cases they may be, but any significant trouble is ultimately going to be psychological in nature and require the proper connection with the Self to outgrow. We have to be wary of anything distracting us from development and transformation, and Jesus knew all too well how incompetent we can be in this area. Many do not have the requisite eyes to see and ears to hear, and many refuse to simply look and listen to things both external and especially internal. That is what Jesus is concerned about here.

Mark 8:23-25 Can you see anything now...Don't even go back to the village first. (heals blind man)

Another healing episode not to be discussed given the context.

Mark 8:27-29 Who do the people think that I am? What are they saying about me?...Who do you think I am? (Peter replies: You are the Messiah)

This is a critical statement from Peter (which he will quickly semi-erase in the next passage) because he is able to perceive Jesus as who he really is. Acknowledging the Self and living accordingly will be met with a positive reflection back from the Self. Also notice that Jesus is most concerned with what each individual thinks regarding his identity; too often we shift attention away from our own issues and direction instead of keeping our eyes and ears where they need to be.

Mark 8:33 Satan, get behind me! You are looking at this only from a human point of view and not from God's (rebukes Peter regarding the cross)

Peter is doing exactly what Jesus says he is doing; we will take up the critical meaning of this passage in Matthew's Gospel.

Mark 8:34-38 If any of you wants to be my follower, you must put aside your own pleasures and take up your cross, and follow me closely. If you insist on saving your life, you will lose it. Only those who throw away their lives for my sake and for the sake of the Good News will ever know what it means to really live. And how does a man benefit if he gains the whole world but loses his soul in the process? For is anything worth more than his soul? And anyone who is ashamed of me and my message in these days of unbelief and sin, I, the Messiah (Son of Man[40]), will

---

40.  This is a reference to the Book of Daniel in the Old Testament, and its meaning will be fully discussed when we reach John's Gospel.

be ashamed of him when I return in the glory of my Father, with the holy angels.

Another key passage; Jesus reminds that *what the ego wants is always subordinate to the mandates of the Self.* If we try to hold on to anything getting in the way of our true identities, development, and transformation, we will not experience the rebirth that is required for growth. We may get trapped by material possessions, money, addictions, psychological disturbances, family ties, etc., but usually the core issue holding us back is some kind of wrong attitude (for example, inflation) towards the Self. We have to die like Jesus, Osiris, the phoenix, etc. if we expect to rise from the ashes and be reborn. This is a process that happens multiple times in our lives and is not to be taken as an isolated occurrence (organized religion take note!), for anything that happens once at a certain historical point and doesn't keep on going is effectively dead.

We all have crosses to carry, and Jesus expects that we do so as well as heed the call of the Self. This is how we save our souls. This is not a popular undertaking for obvious reasons, but it is a necessary one.

Mark 9:1 Some of you who are standing here right now will live to see the Kingdom of God arrive in great power!

It is not immediately clear what Jesus exactly means here, but what is clear is that those with eyes to see and ears to hear will find God in everything both around and within them. The Kingdom is not bound by time and space; it is here and now as well as any time period and area!

Mark 9:16-29 What's all the argument about?...Oh, what tiny faith you have. How much longer must I be with you until you believe? How much longer must I be patient with you? Bring the boy to me...How long has he been this way?...If I can? *Anything* is possible if you have faith. O demon of deafness and dumbness, I command you to come out of the child and enter him no more!...Cases like this require prayer. (Jesus cures the boy)

A balance of faith and reason is required to develop the proper connection to the Self. We cannot fully lean on our own understanding, but we also cannot bury our rationality talents. This is a both/and issue, not an either/or one. Anything is indeed possible with the Self, and in difficult cases and situations, we have to establish connection with the Self (prayer) and be both patient and receptive to what happens. We (the ego) do have limits, and sometimes effort alone cannot heal our troubles.

Mark 9:31 I, the Messiah (Son of Man), am going to be betrayed and killed and three days later will return to life again.

Here is the death and rebirth archetype again. It also shows that Jesus is both fully human and fully divine. Nobody except such an entity could know such things; it would be great if we were 100% sure what will happen when we move towards the ashes, but we do not have this advantage that Jesus had. The three days is a metaphorical, not a literal, time period as well.

Mark 9:33-35 What were you discussing out on the road?... Anyone wanting to be the greatest must be the least-the servant of all!

Jesus is showing here that becoming "great" requires being humble and emptying oneself (Greek: *kenosis*). Both Jesus and Buddha renounced any status they had and emptied themselves in the process. These types of paradoxes are often true in areas of depth.

Narcissism is a key issue here as the Apostles were arguing about who was the greatest among them. Many people think of arrogance when the term narcissism is mentioned, but it is just as much about self-pity as well. Though the two types may seem opposite, they actually both have the common core of self-centeredness and as a result disconnect from others. Going even deeper, narcissism is often at root about *lack of identity*. In the Greek myth of Narcissus, he gets lost in his own reflection in front of the pool, and he wastes away in that state, just like Echo does trying to get him to pay attention to her[41]. It is as if the psyche is attempting to pool (pun intended) its resources inward for the purpose of development and transformation in narcissistic individuals, but it gets bastardized in the ways mentioned above. The direction provided is lost, and Jesus knew well how this works.

Mark 9:37 Anyone who welcomes a child such as this in my name is welcoming me, and anyone who welcomes me is welcoming my Father who sent me!

We have to learn to see Jesus in even the "smallest" of people, and we have to be receptive and open-minded to do so.

Mark 9:39-50 Don't forbid him! For no one doing miracles in my name will quickly turn against me. Anyone who isn't against us is for us. Anyone who so much as gives you a cup of water because you are Christ's-I solemnly say this-he won't lose his reward.

---

41.  see N. Schwartz-Salant: Narcissism and Character Transformation for these points as well as excellent coverage of narcissism.

But if someone causes one of these little ones who believe in me to lose faith-it would be better for that man if a huge millstone were tied to his neck and he were thrown into the sea. If your hand does wrong, cut it off. Better live with one hand than be thrown into the unquenchable fires of hell with two! If your foot carries you towards evil, cut it off. Better be lame and live forever than have two feet that carry you to hell. And if your eye is sinful, gouge it out. Better to enter the Kingdom of God half-blind than have two eyes and see the fires of hell, where the worm never dies, and the fire never goes out-where all are salted with fire. Good salt is worthless if it loses its saltiness; it can't season anything. So don't lose your flavor. Live in peace with each other.

Anything done for the sake of the Self will eventually create growth, and anyone acting in this way will indeed be hard to shake. If we can avoid the numerous traps that set us against the Self in service of the ego, we will be on the correct side of things, as it were. And again, we see how just a bit of energy, represented by the simple gesture of a cup of water, can go a long way. We have to be very careful not to mislead either ourselves or others regarding trusting the guidance of the Self. We can end up in quite the hellish state if we fail here, regardless of the reasons.

The point about the salt is that our essential identity, under the watch of the Self, must not be lost, or no seasoning, which can literally mean maturing/growing, can happen as a person. This lack often leads to states of dis-comfort and dis-ease.

Mark 10:3-12 What did Moses say about divorce?...And why did he say that? I'll tell you why-it was a concession to your hardhearted wickedness. But it certainly isn't God's way. For from the very first he made man and woman to be permanently joined in marriage; therefore a man is to leave his father and mother, and he and his wife are united so they are no longer two, but one. And no man may separate what God has joined together...When a man divorces his wife to marry someone else, he commits adultery against her. And if a wife divorces her husband and remarries, she, too, commits adultery.

Jesus is pointing out the spiritual component that forms the foundation of healthy married relationships. The union of opposites, male and female in this case, results in a transformation in both people that transcends the parts and results in a third, unified state. Commitments (of any kind) are to be honored. These aspects of relationships point out what nature/God envisions in this realm. This does *not* mean that abusive or otherwise unhealthy relationships should be maintained, and with the Moses situation, he was trying to meet the people where they were at that point in that context. Finally, I would point out, as a psychologist, that divorce may be necessary where the proper foundations were/are not present. However, in all cases, the marriage happened; an annulment, for example, is just another form of cancel culture, which ultimately will not be tolerated by nature.

Mark 10:14-15 Let the children come to me, for the Kingdom of God belongs to such as they. Don't send them away! I tell you as seriously as I know how that anyone who refuses to come to God as a little child will never be allowed into his Kingdom.

Connecting to the Cosmic Self/God requires a childlike state of openness to experience and the ability to be humble. No one is anything but infinitesimally small compared to God, and a child's wonder and trust is in order, even though we cannot suppress our abilities in the realm of knowledge.

Mark 10:18-27 Why do you call me good? Only God is truly good! But as for your question-you know the commandments: don't kill, don't commit adultery, don't steal, don't lie, don't cheat, honor your father and mother...You lack only one thing. Go and sell all you have and give the money to the poor-and you shall have treasure in heaven-and come, follow me...It's almost impossible for the rich to get into the Kingdom of God...Dear children, how hard it is for those who trust in riches to enter the Kingdom of God. It is easier for a camel to pass through the eye of a needle than for a rich man to enter the Kingdom of God... Without God, it is utterly impossible. But with God everything is possible.

We have an immediate issue here, as Jesus clearly distinguishes himself from God, which is a blatant contradiction. However, what he says is true. What he doesn't say is also true, but that will have to wait for the appropriate area of John's Gospel, other than to mention here that good is undefinable without evil, just as is true of all pairs of opposites. One doesn't make any sense without the other; there is no comparison or reference point without both. But as to the rest of the content here, Jesus notes how being rich in worldly things is a blockade to true connection with the Self. And it isn't just literally having lots of money, but rather any area that is too much, be it a state of inflation, overreliance on a developed personality area at the expense of an undeveloped one, valuing status or even one's relatives too highly, etc. The primary focus has to be the Self, regardless of what we have or do not have. It is a fair question to wonder how anyone achieves a state of Heaven, Nirvana, or other analog since no one is perfect in these ways. That's why Jesus finishes by noting that without the Self (God), nothing is possible, but with God, anything may be. This discussion about the rich man in the Bible is a powerful lesson for everyone, and personally, I know I have massive work to do regarding letting go of certain pathological coping mechanisms, for example. All of us need to take inventory of where we are in this regard.

Mark 10:29-31 Let me assure you that no one who has ever given up anything-home, brothers, sisters, mother, father, children, or property-for love of me or to tell others the Good News-who won't be given back, a hundred times over, homes, brothers, sisters, mother, father, children, and land-with persecutions! All these will be his here on earth, and in the world to come he shall have eternal life. But many people who seem to be important now will be least important then, and many who are considered least important here shall be greatest there.

So much of what Jesus preaches is paradoxical but true, and that is the case here. Only by letting go or letting be do we actually gain (transformation and growth). What is valuable from our point of view (ego) may be of little importance to the eye of God (Self).

Mark 10:33-34 When we get there, I, the Messiah, will be taken before the chief priests and Jewish leaders, who will sentence me to die and hand me over to the Romans to be killed. They will mock me and spit on me and flog me with their whips and kill me, but in three days I will come back to life again.

Jesus predicts his passion and resurrection. This is not a one-time event, as Christian dogma states, but dying and rising at a new level is constantly happening, or at least we are faced with the Cross in this way, as Jesus said we would be, many times. If this is isolated to one event in history, then there is no more life in it, and we know from experience and other data that both God and we are living entities confronted with the cycle of death and rebirth that is the way of nature.

Mark 10:36-40 What is it?... You do not know what you are asking! Are you able to drink from the bitter cup of sorrow that I must drink from? Or to be baptized with the baptism of suffering I must be baptized with?...Indeed you will drink from my cup and be baptized with my baptism, but I do not have the right to place you on thrones next to mine. Those appointments have already been made.

This passage basically repeats the previous one; what happened to Jesus will also happen with us. Transformation cannot take place without the death of old, worn out ways of being. I do not think we can know the nature of the "appointments" that Jesus says have already been made or to whom or what they pertain, and it certainly is again odd that Jesus would not have the right to do such a thing. Predestination runs contrary to both Jesus' messages and depth psychology, among other areas, so these already-filled thrones are somewhat of an enigma, especially if one believes in free will, choices, etc. My take is that we just need to keep the ego-Self axis in healthy working order, and we'll reach the state we strive to attain. But Jesus is absolutely correct that most have no idea what they are asking in this context. This type of psychological/spiritual work is the hardest kind there is.

> This great symbol tells us that the progressive development
> and differentiation of consciousness leads to an ever more
> menacing awareness of the conflict and involves nothing less
> than a crucifixion of the ego, its agonizing suspension between
> irreconcilable opposites. (C.G. Jung)[42]

Mark 10:42-46 As you know, the kings and great men of the earth lord it over the people, but among you it is different. Whoever wants to be the great among you must be your servant. And whoever wants to be the greatest of all must be the servant of all. For even I, the Messiah, am not here to be served, but to help others, and to give my life as a ransom for many.

Again, the paradoxical truths, combined with sacrificing for the sake of development and transformation.

Mark 10:49-52 Tell him (blind Bartamaeus) to come here...What do you want me to do for you?...All right, it's done. Your faith has healed you.

This is another healing episode, but it shows that connection with the Self allows one to see necessary things of which we would not otherwise be aware.

Mark 11:2:3 Go into that village over there...and just as you enter you will see a colt tied up that has never been ridden. Untie him and bring him here. And if anyone asks you what you are doing, just say, 'Our Master has need of him and will return him soon.'

Jesus will ride into Jerusalem on Palm Sunday in quite the humble manner. We could learn a thing or two here.

Mark 11:14 You shall never bear fruit again! (cursed fig tree)

---

42.   C.G. Jung – Aion - [CW 9(II), para. 79, p. 44]

It certainly is unusual for Jesus to curse something in this way, but I read this event as a lesson showing that if we keep the wrong conscious attitude and approach to development and transformation in context of the Self, we cannot be fruitful. Therefore, "never again" would apply to the stubbornness we show by being under the wrong cross, as it were. We could potentially change that...

Mark 11:17 It is written in the Scriptures, My Temple is to be a place of prayer for all nations, but you have turned it into a den of robbers!

This is the well-known episode where Jesus overturns the tables in the Temple out of righteous anger. The territory of the Self must be respected, or it will strike back, often by way of karma. I believe we are literally seeing membership in any organized religion drop dramatically, thereby overturning these institutions, because they have strayed so far from what Jesus and the other leaders intended.

Mark 11:22-25 If you only have faith in God-this is the absolute truth-you can say to this Mount of Olives, 'Rise up and fall into the Mediterranean,' and it will obey your command. All that's required is that you really believe and have no doubt! Listen to me! You can pray for *anything, and if you really believe, you have it, it's yours!* But when you are praying, first forgive anyone you are holding a grudge against, so your Father in heaven may forgive your sins too.

Faith in the Self indeed creates "miraculous" things. And of course we cannot be hypocrites and expect that we will experience forgiveness if we cannot or will not forgive others.

As for prayer, it is always useful to communicate with God, but God isn't going to simply grant anything we wish. We also have no right to demand anything from God in most cases, even if it seems like we somehow deserve it. What should be prayed for is development and transformation, because that is both necessary and hugely fruitful.

Mark 11:29-33 I'll tell you if you answer one question! Was John the Baptist sent by God? Was he sent by God or not? Answer me! ....Then I won't answer your question either!

Jesus isn't having these types of games, not one bit.

Mark 12:1-11 A man planted a vineyard and built a wall around it and dug a pit for pressing out the grape juice, and built a watchman's tower. Then he leased the farm to tenant farmers and moved to another country. At grape-picking time he sent one of his men to collect his share of the crop. But the farmers beat up the man and sent him back empty-handed. The owner then sent another of his men, who received the same treatment, only worse, for his head was seriously injured. The next man he sent was killed; and later, others were beaten or killed, until there was only one left-his only son. He finally sent him, thinking they would give him their full respect. But when the farmers saw him coming they said, 'He will own the farm when his father dies. Come on, let's kill him-and then the farm will be ours! So they caught him and murdered him and threw his body out of the vineyard. What do you suppose the owner will do when he hears what happened? He will come and kill them all, and lease the vineyard to others. Don't you remember reading this verse in the Scriptures? **The Rock the builders threw away became**

**the cornerstone**, the most honored stone in the building! This is the Lord's doing and it is an amazing thing to see.

Obviously, one cannot get away with such behavior without karma eventually hitting hard, and nature shows us the face we show it. If we judge that another's life can be taken, then so too shall we be judged. Not much analysis is needed here. However, the proverbial *stone that the builders rejected* refers to Jesus, the Philosopher's Stone in alchemy, and other such entities. This is exactly the way the archetypal psyche (God) acts; what appears cheap and worthless is actually the foundation and most important thing. For example, Jesus, Buddha, and the Philosopher's Stone all appear to have little value by worldly standards, but the exact opposite is true.

**Mark 12:15-17 Show me a coin and I'll tell you...Whose picture is this on the coin?...All right, (he said), if it is his, give it to him. but everything that belongs to God must be given to God.**

This is the give Caesar what's Caesar's and God what is God's message. Sorry to anyone who thought taxes could be avoided! But this is a great verse when we have work we do not want to do or seems (and may be) pointless. It is also good when there is a price to pay for some goal or when we have to admit we were wrong. There are many applications of this passage, but those pertaining to the Self must be primary.

**Mark 12:24-27 Your trouble is that you don't know the Scriptures, and don't know the power of God. For when these seven brothers and the woman rise from the dead, they won't be married-they will be like the angels. But now as to whether there will be a resurrection-have you never read in the book of Exodus**

about Moses and the burning bush? God said to Moses, 'I *am* the God of Abraham, and I *am* the God of Isaac, and I *am* the God of Jacob.' God was telling Moses that these men, though dead for hundreds of years, were still very much alive for he would not have said, 'I *am* the God' of those who don't exist! You have made a serious error.

The comment about marriage is a bit off our focus here, but the general idea is that (at least in the East) we become part of the cosmic union of (male and female) opposites in the end. This idea is also expressed regarding those who pass from this life becoming part of the Force in Star Wars. But, the "I am" comment is key; death is really a transition to another mode of existence, and God is both living and unbound by time and space. That's what Jesus means here.

Mark 12:29-31 The one that says, 'Hear, O Israel! The Lord our God is the one and only God. And you must love him with all your heart and soul and mind and strength.' The second is: 'you must love others as much as yourself.' No other commandments are greater than these.

The Self is primary, and we are made in the image and likeness of God. Therefore, these would be the two greatest commandments.

Mark 12:34 You are not far from the Kingdom of God.

This is true when we pattern our lives by the Self, but the experience may initially be painful.

Mark 12:35-37 Why do your religious teachers claim that the Messiah must be a descendant of King David? For David himself said-and the Holy Spirit was speaking through him when he said it-'God said to my lord, sit at my right hand until I make your enemies your footstool.' Since David called him his lord, how can he be his *son*?

David cannot be shown to be Jesus' literal father, though the historical Jesus is considered to be from David's line. This is one of many areas where getting caught in literal details at the expense of meaning creates issues. The nature of Jesus and what he symbolizes from the Christian perspective is what matters.

Mark 12:38-40 **Beware of the teachers of religion! For they love to wear the robes of the rich and scholarly, and to have everyone bow to them as they walk through the markets. They love to sit in the best seats in the synagogues, and at the places of honor at banquets-but they shamelessly cheat widows out of their homes and then, to cover up the kind of men they really are, they pretend to be pious by praying long prayers in public.** Because of this, their punishment will be the greater.

All I can say here is that clergy of any religion, especially the hypocrites and misguided ones, take note!

Mark 12:43-44 That poor widow has given more than all those rich men put together! For they gave a little of their extra fat, while she gave up her last penny.

We have to be all-in with development and transformation in context of the Self. There is no literal amount of energy required, just 100% of what we can give. That is also a direct parallel to the quantum leap in chemistry/physics with electrons jumping to the next energy state; it requires 100% of the necessary energy to occur.

Mark 13:2 Yes, look! For not one stone will be left upon another, except as ruins.

Nothing in the space-time frame lasts forever.

Mark 13:5-37 Don't let anyone mislead you, for many will come declaring themselves to be our Messiah, and will lead many astray. And wars will break out near and far, but this is not the signal of the end-time. For nations and kingdoms will proclaim war against each other, and there will be earthquakes in many lands, and famines. These herald only the early stages of the anguish ahead. But when these things begin to happen, watch out! For you will be in great danger. You will be dragged before the courts, and beaten in the synagogues, and accused before governors and kings of being my followers. This is your opportunity to tell them the Good News. And the Good News must first be made known in every nation before the end-time finally comes. But when you are arrested and stand trial, don't worry about what to say in your defense. Just say what God tells you to. Then you will not be speaking, but the Holy Spirit will. Brothers will betray each other to death, fathers will betray their own children, and children will betray their parents to be killed. **And everyone will hate you because you are mine. But all who endure to the end without renouncing me shall be saved.** When you see the horrible thing standing in the Temple-reader, pay attention-flee, if you can, to the Judean hills. Hurry! If you are on your rooftop porch, don't even go back into the house. If you are out in the fields, don't even return for your money or clothes. Woe to pregnant women in those days, or to mothers nursing their children. And pray that your flight will not be in winter. For those will be the days of horror as have never been seen since the beginning of God's creation, nor will ever be again. And unless the Lord shortens the time of the calamity, not a soul in all the earth will survive. But for the sake of his chosen ones he will limit those days. And then if anyone tells you 'This is the Messiah', or, 'That one is', don't pay any attention. For there will be many false prophets who will do wonderful miracles that will deceive, if possible, even God's own children. Take care! I have warned you! And when the tribulation ends, the sun will grow dim and the moon will not shine. And the stars will fall- the heavens will convulse. Then you will see me, the Messiah, coming in the clouds with great power and glory. And I will send out the angels to gather together my chosen ones from all over the world-from the farthest bounds of earth and heaven. Now here is a lesson from a fig tree. When its buds become tender and its leaves begin to sprout, you know spring has come. And when you see these things happening that I've described, you can be sure that my return is very near, that I am right at the door. Yes, these are the events that will signal the end of the age. Heaven and earth shall disappear, but my words stand sure forever. However, no one, not the angels in heaven, nor I myself, knows the day or hour these things will happen, only the Father knows. Since you do not know when these things will happen, stay alert. Be on the watch [for my return]. My return can be compared to that of a man who went to another country. He laid out his employees' work for them to do while he was gone, and told the gatekeeper to watch for his return. Keep a sharp lookout, for you do not know if I will come at evening, midnight, early dawn, or daybreak. Don't let me find you sleeping. *Watch for my return!* This is my message to you and to everyone else.

This the apocalyptic chapter of Mark's Gospel, but again, while these things are in the future, they are also *now*, and the fabric of reality has nothing to do with time and space anyway except in very tiny part. And nobody can predict when things will "end." There always have been and always will be false prophets, but the truth stands sure as Jesus notes. The key is to follow the guidance of the Self (for which you may be hated) and increase conscious awareness, development, and transformation so that you are ready and not asleep, as it were. Whoever does this and endures the tension of opposites will indeed be saved.

Mark 14:6-9 Let her alone; why berate her for doing a good thing? You always have the poor among you, and they badly need your help, and you can aid them whenever you want to; but I won't be here much longer. She has done what she could, and anointed my body for burial ahead of time. And I tell you this in solemn truth, that wherever the Good News is preached throughout the world, this woman's deed will be remembered and praised.

This woman's use of expensive oils to anoint Jesus may appear foolish from the perspective of the ego, but any energy paid towards the Self will be remembered for eternity.

Mark 14:13-16 As you are walking along, you will see a man coming towards you carrying a pot of water. Follow him. At the house he enters, tell the man in charge, 'Our Master sent us to see the room you have ready for us, where we will eat the Passover supper this evening!' He will take you to a large room upstairs all set up. Prepare our supper there.

Jesus is preparing the environment where he will share his body and blood. More on this later...

Mark 14:18-21 I solemnly declare that one of you will betray me, one of you who is here eating with me...it is one of you twelve eating with me here now. I must die, as the prophets declared long ago; but oh, the misery ahead for the man by whom I am betrayed. Oh, that he had never been born!

Judas actually repents for what he did, but one can imagine the guilt and shame that karma would bring for such an act. And how often do we betray the Self by our attitudes and actions? Probably more than we would like to admit…

Mark 14:22-25 Eat it-this is my body…this is my blood, poured out for many, sealing the new agreement between God and man. I solemnly declare that I shall never taste wine again until the day I drink a different kind in the Kingdom of God.

Everything, including wine, would be different in the Kingdom. But there is such great argument among Christian denominations about whether or not it is literally the body and blood of Christ. In reality, the wrong issue is being considered, so all denominations are at least partially wrong because they've again fallen into the trap of focusing on the literal when the real issue is the meaning. And the meaning is actually more real than anything literal here: the bond between human and divine in evolved form (ego-Self axis). The custom of eating/drinking the god is an ancient idea that predates Christianity, and whether it is literal or not frankly doesn't matter. It is accurate to call it symbolic, because archetypal transformations were at work here as well as today, but the meaning as stated is true and what matters. And yet Christianity persists in dividing itself over the wrong issue. I believe someone important said a house divided cannot stand, and I am certain the reader knows who said that. He also said we have to stop thinking like humans (the ego) do, hard as it may be.

Mark 14:27-28 All of you will desert me, for God has declared through the prophets, 'I will kill the Shepherd, and the sheep will scatter. But after I am raised to life again, I will go to Galilee and meet you there.'

How hard it is to stay true to the Self when it appears to or actually deserts you! Even Peter cannot do it. But the Self can be trusted to be there and to return if it abandons you, just as Jesus, who is its symbol for Christians, does.

Mark 14:30 Peter, before the cock crows a second time tomorrow morning you will deny me three times.

Peter thinks he is somehow exempt from the previous passage. Wrong. Nobody can be totally sure how he or she will act until faced with said situation in reality. Stanley Milgram's famous shock experiments showed this in a laboratory setting, and there is a reason that what actually happened in Nazi Germany and other such places (e.g. Rwanda in the 1990s) is so often connected to these experiments. People struggle mightily to act properly in the face of things like authority, hardship, etc. Never assume; it makes an ass out of u and me.

Mark 14:32 Sit here, while I go and pray.

What is about to happen to Jesus is the type of thing that cannot be endured without a living connection to the Self (established by prayer here).

Mark 14:34 My soul is crushed by sorrow to the point of death; stay here and watch with me.

Companionship and awareness are so important when faced with an impending apocalyptic moment.

Mark 14:36 Father, Father, everything is possible for you. Take away this cup from me. But I want your will, not mine.

This shows how we should pray: for God's will, not for things or outcomes we desire.

Mark 14:37 Simon, asleep? Couldn't you even watch with me one hour? Watch and pray with me, lest the Tempter overpower you. For though the spirit is willing enough, the body is weak.

Jesus shows his human side here, though it is not exactly human as we are, even though that's what dogma teaches. He knew who he was and what would happen at every point, and this is not true for us. If you think you do, there are plenty of professionals who could see you...

Mark 14:41-42 Sleep on; get your rest! But no! The time for sleep has ended! Look! I am betrayed into the hands of wicked men. Come! Get up! We must go! Look! My betrayer is here!

His hour has come! Are we getting ready for ours?

Mark 14:48-49 Am I some dangerous robber, that you come like this, armed to the teeth to capture me? Why didn't you arrest me in the temple? I was there teaching every day. But these things are happening to fulfill the prophecies about me.

Jesus was a threat to the establishment, so they come armed and will kill him. But such actions will always fail in the end if they try to do this in error, which they are doing. This happens to people who upend the status quo today as well.

Mark 14:62 I am, and you will see me seated at the right hand of God, and returning to earth in the clouds of heaven. (in response to the High Priest)

Not what the establishment wanted to hear…

Mark 15:2 Yes, it is as you say. (in response to Pilate asking if he was King of the Jews)

Pilate was more reasonable than some, but he just tried to wash his hands of it all. How well did that work out for, say, Lady MacBeth of Shakesperian lore?

Mark 15:34 Eli, Eli, lama sabachthani? (**My God, my God, why have you deserted me?**)[43]

Jesus breathes his last…

Mark 16:15-18 You are to go into all the world and preach the Good News to everyone, everywhere. Those who believe and are baptized will be saved. But those who refuse to believe will be condemned. And those who believe shall use my authority to cast out demons, and they shall speak new languages. They will be able even to handle snakes with safety, and if they drink anything poisonous, it won't hurt them; and they will be able to place their hands on the sick and heal them.

Because he was willing to die and be reborn, Jesus has achieved great development and transformation, which he will pass on via the Holy Spirit. We are to follow his lead, but in our own ways. *We are here to live our lives, not Jesus' life.* If we can accomplish this development and transformation via conscious awareness, death, and rebirth on a new level, we do gain this type of authority. Our very being speaks for itself. Like Gandhi said, "Be the change you wish to see in the world." This gain, as Jesus says, is meant for *everyone.*

---

43.  see also Psalm 22

## Matthew (Symbol: Divine Man)

Matthew's Gospel is the longest of the four and includes a geneaology of Jesus' ancestors at the beginning. It is also famously known for Jesus' Sermon on the Mount.

Matthew 3:15 Please do it, for I must do all that is right. (Jesus asks John the Baptist to baptize him)

Even Jesus knows he must do what is required to fulfill his purpose, and so must we.

Matthew 3:17 This is my beloved Son, and I am wonderfully pleased with him. (after Jesus' baptism; said by the Father)

The Cosmic Self introduces Jesus, and as it is said, to "listen to him." It is always a good idea to pay attention to an incarnation of the Self.

Matthew 4:4-10 (Jesus tempted) No! For the Scriptures tell us that bread won't feed men's souls: obedience to every word of God is what we need...It also says not to put the Lord your God to a foolish test!...Get out of here, Satan. The Scriptures say, 'Worship only the Lord God. Obey only him.'

There are always temptations and distractions that pull us away from identity and meaning in context of the Self. This is the ultimate authority to which the ego must pay attention. The interpretation of Satan would be anything keeping us away from the associated development and transformation. However, notice the wording "foolish test." When we discuss Job in context of John's Gospel and overall, we will see that there are legitimate tests for God and that Jesus is eventually the result of what Job demanded: a fair trial before the deity.

Matthew 4:17 Turn from sin, and turn to God, for the Kingdom of heaven is near.

This passage has the same meaning as in Mark (and as suggested above).

Matthew 4:19 Come along with me and I will show you how to fish for the souls of men!

The Self is a wonderful guide in finding out your identity and purpose and helping others to find theirs.

Matthew 5:3-10 Humble men are very fortunate! For the Kingdom of Heaven is given to them. Those who mourn are fortunate! For they shall be comforted. The meek and lowly are fortunate! For the whole wide world belongs to them. Happy are those who long to be just and good, for they shall be completely satisfied. Happy are the kind and merciful, for they shall be shown mercy. Happy are those whose hearts are pure, for they shall see God. Happy are those who strive for peace-they shall be called the sons of God. Happy are those who are persecuted because they are good, for the Kingdom of Heaven is theirs.

This is Jesus' famous Sermon on the Mount. Yes, he was speaking to oppressed people, but the psychology here is solid. Jung speaks everywhere about the concept of *enantiodromia*, or conversion into the opposite. That is exactly what Jesus is illustrating here. Anything in life can flip, suddenly or slowly, so the best approach is to try to follow the Self and keep the middle level regarding thinking and emotions, just like Odysseus did going right between Scylla and Charybdis and by hearing the Sirens (shadow psychological material, complexes, etc.) via tying himself to his ship's mast and having the sailors plug their ears[44]. Solid foundations and evenness matter in life. Furthermore, anyone who is very far to one end or another in most areas is more likely to have an enantiodromia occur; the strong presence of one pole means the other is likely equally strong either in the unconscious or in reality. This concept is also supported by Newton's law of equal and opposite reactions to all actions.

Every psychological extreme secretly contains its own opposite or stands in some sort of intimate and essential relation to it. Indeed, it is from this tension that it derives its peculiar dynamism. There is no hallowed custom that cannot on occasion turn into its opposite, and the more extreme a position is, the more easily may we expect an enantiodromia, a conversion of something into its opposite. (C.G. Jung)[45]

Matthew 5:11-48 When you are reviled and persecuted and lied about because you are my followers-wonderful! Be *happy* about it! Be *very glad*! For a *tremendous reward* awaits you up in heaven. And remember, the ancient prophets were persecuted too. You are the world's seasoning, to make it tolerable. If you lose your flavor, what will happen to the world? And you yourselves will be thrown out and trampled underfoot as worthless. You are the world's light-a city on a hill, glowing in the night for all to see. Don't hide your light! Let it shine for all; let your good deeds glow for all to see, so that they will

---

44.  see E.F. Edinger - The Eternal Drama: The Inner Meaning of Greek Mythology
45.  from C.G. Jung – Symbols of Transformation, p. 375 [CW 5, para. 581]

praise your heavenly Father. Don't misunderstand why I have come-it isn't to cancel the laws of Moses and the warnings of the prophets. No, I came to fulfill them, and to make them all come true. With all the earnestness I have I say: Every law in the Book will continue until its purpose is achieved. And so if anyone breaks the least commandment, and teaches others to, he shall be the least in the Kingdom of Heaven. But those who teach God's laws *and obey them* shall be great in the Kingdom of Heaven. But I warn you-unless your goodness is greater than that of the Pharisees and other Jewish leaders, you can't get into the Kingdom of Heaven at all! Under the law of Moses, the rule was, 'If you kill, you must die.' But I have added to that rule, and tell you that if you are only *angry*, even in your own home, you are in danger of judgment! If you call your friend an idiot, you are in danger of being brought before the court. And if you curse him, you are in danger of the fires of hell. So if you are standing before the altar in the Temple, offering a sacrifice to God, and suddenly remember that a friend has something against you, leave your sacrifice there beside the altar and go and apologize and be reconciled to him, and then come and offer your sacrifice to God. Come to terms quickly with your enemy before it is too late and he drags you into court and you are thrown into a debtor's cell, for you will stay there until you have paid the last penny. The laws of Moses said, 'You shall not commit adultery.' But I say: Anyone who even looks at a woman with lust in his eye has already committed adultery with her in his heart. So if your eye-even if it is your best eye-causes you to lust, gouge it out and throw it away. Better for part of you to be destroyed than for all of you to be cast into hell. And if your hand-even your right hand-causes you to sin, cut it off and throw it away. Better that than find yourself in hell. The law of Moses says, 'If anyone wants to be rid of his wife, he can divorce her merely by giving her a letter of dismissal.' But I say that a man who divorces his wife, except for fornication, causes her to commit adultery if she marries again. And he who marries her commits adultery. Again, the law of Moses says, 'You shall not break your vows to God, but must fulfill them all.' But I say: Don't make any vows! And even to say, 'By heavens!' is a sacred vow to God, for the heavens are God's throne. And if you say, 'By the earth!', it is a sacred vow, for the earth is his footstool. And don't swear 'By Jerusalem!', for Jerusalem is the capital of the great king. Don't even swear 'By my head!', for you can't turn one hair white or black. Say just a simple 'Yes I will' or 'No, I won't.' Your word is enough. To strengthen your promise with a vow shows that something is wrong. The law of Moses says, 'If a man gouges out another's eye, he must pay with his own eye. If a tooth gets knocked out, knock out the tooth of the one who did it.' But I say: Don't resist violence! If you are slapped on one cheek, turn the other too. If you are ordered to court, and your shirt is taken from you, give your coat too. If the military demand that you carry their gear for a mile, carry it two. Give to those who ask, and don't turn away from those who want to borrow. There is a saying, 'Love your *friends* and hate your enemies.' But I say: Love your *enemies*! Pray for those who persecute you! In that way you will be acting as true sons of your Father in heaven. For he gives his sunlight to both the evil and the good, and sends rain on the just and on the unjust too. If you love only those who love you, what good is that? Even scoundrels do that much. If you are friendly only to your friends, how are you different from anyone else? Even the heathen do that. But you are to be perfect, even as your Father in heaven is perfect.

There is a lot here, so let's break it down. As noted earlier, standing up for the values of the Self often has a price, but the reward is (eventually) great. We are to embrace light (consciousness, talents, etc.) and be the flavoring salt previously discussed in Mark's Gospel. And, every law directed by the Self, including even some human-made laws, must be fulfilled.

Swearing in this context refers to placing authority where it doesn't belong (away from the Self). What attitudes and behaviors must we cut away, as Jesus notes, to stay true in this area? For one thing, we certainly cannot be hypocrites (like the Pharisees, Sadducees, Jewish leaders, etc.), though we all are from time to time, especially when complexes (remember they are essentially unhealthy programmed responses to shadow areas with an archetypal core underlying them) are involved. And if we cannot love our enemies, how can we ever withdraw our own projections we have placed on them or expect mercy ourselves? The well-known phrase "turn the other cheek" actually was a way of demanding respect and dignity in those times[46], so Jesus didn't expect people to simply take abuse, though he didn't condone the retributive justice[47] that many seek. Finally, when Jesus says to be perfect like the Father, we can shift "perfect" to "complete" and get an accurate read on how he meant the statement to be taken.

---

46.  D. Hocoy, personal communication, Pacifica Graduate Institute.
47.  see R. Rohr, Daily Meditation emails, CAC.

Matthew 6:1-34 Take care! Don't do your good deeds publicly, to be admired, for then you will lose the reward from your Father in heaven. When you give a gift to a beggar, don't shout about it as the hypocrites do-blowing trumpets in the synagogues and streets to call attention to their acts of charity! I tell you in all earnestness, they have received all the reward they will ever get. But when you do a kindness to someone, do it secretly-don't tell your left hand what your right hand is doing. And your Father who knows all secrets will reward you. And now about prayer. When you pray, don't be like the hypocrites who pretend piety by praying publicly on street corners and in the synagogues where everyone can see them. Truly, that is all the reward they will ever get. But when you pray, go away by yourself, all alone, and shut the door behind you and pray to your Father secretly, and your Father, who knows your secrets, will reward you. Don't recite the same prayer over and over as the heathen do, who think prayers are answered only by repeating them again and again. Remember, your Father knows exactly what you need even before you ask him! (Our Father taught) Pray along these lines: **'Our Father in heaven, we honor your holy name. We ask that your kingdom will come now. May your will be done here on earth, just as it is in heaven. Give us our food again today, as usual, and forgive us our sins, just as we have forgiven those who have sinned against us. Don't bring us into temptation, but deliver us from the Evil One. Amen.'** Your heavenly Father will forgive you if you forgive those who sin against you, but if *you* refuse to forgive *them, he* will not forgive *you.* And now about fasting. When you fast, declining your food for a spiritual purpose, don't do it publicly, as the hypocrites do, who try to look wan and disheveled so people will feel sorry for them. Truly, that is the only reward they will ever get. But when you fast, put on festive clothing, so that no one will suspect you are hungry, except your Father who knows every secret. And he will reward you. Don't store up treasures here on earth where they can erode away or may be stolen. Store them in heaven where they will never lose their value, and are safe from thieves. If your profits are in heaven your heart will be there too. If your eye is pure, there will be sunshine in your soul. But if your eye is clouded with evil thoughts and desires, you are in deep spiritual darkness. And oh, how deep that darkness can be! **You cannot serve two masters: God and money.** For you will hate one and love the other, or else the other way around. So my counsel is: Don't worry about things-food, drink, and clothes. For you already have life and a body-and they are far more important than what to eat and wear. Look at the birds! They don't worry about what to eat-they don't need to sow or reap or store up food-for your heavenly Father feeds them. And you are far more valuable to him than they are. Will all your worries add a single moment to your life? And why worry about your clothes? Look at the field lilies! They don't worry about theirs. Yet King Solomon in all his glory was not clothed as beautifully as they. And if God cares so wonderfully for flowers that are here today and gone tomorrow, won't he more surely care for you, O men of little faith? So don't worry at all about having enough food and clothing. Why be like the heathen? For they take pride in all these things and are deeply concerned about them. But your heavenly Father already knows perfectly well that you need them, and he will give them to you if you give him first place in your life and live as he wants you to.

So don't be anxious about tomorrow. God will take care of your tomorrow too. Live one day at a time.

Acting and praying in secret is viewed by Jesus as a virtue here, and the idea is that seeking recognition or the like for such things is vain. If you have to announce it, you probably aren't sincere about or comfortable with whatever the issue is, in addition to potentially functioning in a narcissistic way. Jesus gives us the greatest Christian prayer here, the Our Father, and it reflects everything we have said to this point with the exception of the end, which we will elaborate upon in context of the coming discussion of Job (and others) in John's Gospel.

Our treasure will be where our heart is, and here Jesus mentions one of his more well-known ideas. Putting stock in ego-based desires at the expense of those of the Self is not storing treasure in the right area, as it were. This also connects to the directive not to invest too much energy in (material) things. The comment about proper vision (eye) is the entire point of this book, in a sense. This requires conscious awareness.

We have all heard the idea of two masters. Occasionally, you can have your cake and eat it too, if it is in a healthy context. However, we cannot serve the ego at the expense of the Self. Finally, sufficient are the worries of today, as the saying goes. We cannot play the "what-if game" or get too far ahead at the expense of the present moment, not to mention that how we navigate every step along the way affects subsequent steps, so getting way ahead of ourselves cannot work accurately anyway.

Matthew 7:1-27 Don't criticize, and then you won't be criticized. For others will treat you as you treat them. And why worry about a speck in the eye of a brother when you have a board in your own? Should you say, 'Friend, let me help you get that speck out of your eye,' when you can't even see because of the board in your own? Hypocrite! First get rid of the board. Then you can see to help your brother. Don't give holy thing to depraved men. **Don't give pearls to swine! They will trample the pearls and turn and attack you.** Ask, and you will be given what you ask for. Seek, and you will find. Knock, and the door will be opened. For everyone who asks, receives. Anyone who seeks, finds. If only you will knock, the door will open. If a child asks his father for a loaf of bread, will he be given a stone instead? If he asks for fish, will he be given a poisonous snake? Of course not! And if you hardhearted, sinful men know how to give good gifts to your children, won't your Father in heaven even more certainly give good gifts to those who ask him for them? Do for others what you want them to do for you. This is the teaching of the laws of Moses in a nutshell. **Heaven can be entered only through the narrow gate!** The highway to hell is broad, and its gate is wide enough for all the multitudes who choose its easy way. But the Gateway to Life is small, and the road is narrow, and only a few ever find it. Beware of false teachers who come disguised as harmless sheep, but are wolves and will tear you apart. You can detect them by the way they act, just as you can identify a tree by its fruit. You need never confuse grapevines with thorn bushes or figs with thistles. Different kinds of fruit trees can quickly be identified by examining their fruit. A variety that produces delicious fruit never produces an inedible kind. And a tree producing an inedible kind can't produce what is good. So the trees having the inedible fruit are chopped down and thrown on the fire. Yes, the way to identify a tree or a person is by the kind of fruit produced. Not all who sound religious are really godly people. They may refer to me as 'Lord,' but still won't get to heaven. For the decisive question is whether they obey my Father in heaven. At the Judgment many will tell me, 'Lord, Lord, we told others about you and used your name to cast out demons and to do many other great miracles.' But I will reply, 'You have never been mine. Go away, for your deeds are evil.' **All who listen to my instructions and follow them are wise, like a man who builds his house on solid rock. Though the rain comes in torrents, and the floods rise and the storm winds beat against his house, it won't collapse, for it is built on rock. But those who hear my instructions and ignore them are foolish, like a man who builds his house on sand.** For when the rains and floods come, and storm winds beat against his house, it will fall with a mighty crash.

There are critical points in this section of Matthew's Gospel. The first point is quite direct: take care of your own issues before trying to poke at others' problems. It is usually projection anyway, and the trick is to treat the annoying person as a mirror in which to see some aspect(s) of yourself and take back the projection(s), developing your personality in the process.

> Everything that irritates us about others can lead us to an understanding of ourselves. (C.G. Jung)[48]

The next issue is throwing things of value or meaning at those who do not or cannot appreciate them; doing this will result in

---

48.   from C.G. Jung – Memories, Dreams, Reflections

a backfire where the receiver fails to accept what is offered and may even attack you for bringing the area up! The state of the observer affects the observed. Do not throw pearls of any kind at those not ready to receive them.

Next, asking is required to get an answer, but we have to take care to request things that foster development and transformation and that serve the will of the Self, not the will of the ego. I will go a step further than the Golden Rule mentioned here and note the Platinum Rule, where we treat others the way *they* would like to be treated (provided it is reasonable and appears to be in line with their identities and purposes).

The gate to the state Christians call Heaven is indeed very narrow. Alchemy, via one of its well-known figures, says the same thing as Jesus:

> Exceeding narrow is the gateway to peace, and
> none may enter save through affliction of the soul.
> (Morienus, as cited by Jung)[49]

Following the guidance of the Self is the narrow way, and it involves deep suffering. *The issue is whether or not the suffering is neurotic or transformational, and that depends on the conscious attitude.* And, of course, actions always speak louder than words, so you have to pay attention to the way people act, implicitly or explicitly, not to what they say alone. Finally, building one's house on rock is establishing a foundation based on the Self, which is all about shadow and complex work, completeness, development, and transformation, as opposed to putting stock

---

49.   from C.G. Jung – Psychology and Alchemy (CW 12)

in fleeting or misguided aims of the ego in whatever forms they may take, from stubbornness to alcohol/drugs and everything in between.

Matthew 8:3-4 I want to. Be healed. (a leper)...Don't stop to talk to anyone: go right over to the priest to be examined; and take with you the offering required by Moses' law for lepers who are healed-a public testimony of your cure.

This episode's meaning was noted in our discussion of Mark's Gospel.

Matthew 8:7-13 (Roman army captain) I will come and heal him...I haven't seen faith like this in all the land of Israel! And I tell you this, that many Gentiles [like this Roman officer], shall come from all over the world and sit down in the Kingdom of Heaven with Abraham, Isaac, and Jacob. And many an Israelite-those for whom the Kingdom was prepared-shall be cast into outer darkness, to the place of weeping and torment...Go on home. What you have believed has happened!

Having faith is mentioned often in the Gospels, and the quantum physics principle of the observer affecting the observed is relevant here, as illustrated by the line about what we believe happening. The psychological state we are in will affect us along with everyone and everything around us. And again, an outsider gets it right.

Matthew 8:20-32 Foxes live in dens and birds have nests, but I, the Messiah, have no home of my own-no place to lay my head... Follow me now! Let those who are spiritually dead care for their own dead...O you men of little faith! Why are you so frightened?... All right. Be gone (demons cast into pigs)

Jesus isn't bound to anything except his individuation process and teleological purpose. As the Christian symbol of the Self, this should be the case, as those are the aims of the Self. This is where our attention must be as well. We also have the episode where Jesus sends the demons into pigs. Not the best way to treat animals, but in the context of what happened, getting the shadow areas and complexes resolved apparently required some form of divine intervention at least to this extent, so it was done.

Matthew 9:2-13 Cheer up, son! For I have forgiven your sins!... Why are you thinking such evil thoughts? I, the Messiah, have the authority on earth to forgive sins. But talk is cheap-anybody could say that. So I'll prove it to you by healing this man. Pick up your stretcher and go on home, for you are healed...Come and be my disciple (to Matthew)....Because people who are well don't need a doctor! It's the sick people who do!...Now go away and learn the meaning of this verse of Scripture, 'It isn't your sacrifices and your gifts I want-I want you to be merciful.' For I have come to urge sinners, not the self-righteous, back to God.

We see some themes here that we have already examined as well as Jesus doing what he does. The point about mercy is key, because we all need it, especially those who are very lost. However, this is a two-way street; there is a benefit to God in caring for the worst of the worst. Another important area where the truth is found in terms of both/and, not either/or. We will elaborate on this in our discussion of John's Gospel.

Matthew 9:15-17 Should the bridegroom's friends mourn and go without food while he is with them? But the time is coming when I will be taken from them. Time enough then for them to refuse to eat. And who would patch an old garment with unshrunk cloth? For the patch would tear away and make the hole worse. And who would use old wineskins to store new wine? For the old skins would burst with the pressure, and the wine would be spilled and the skins ruined. Only new wineskins are used to store new wine. That way both are preserved.

Everything evolves or perishes, and that requires a new container that can hold the higher level of development and transformation.

Matthew 9:22-38 Daughter, all is well! Your faith has healed you... Get them out, for the little girl isn't dead; she is only sleeping!...Do you believe I can make you see?...Because of your faith it will happen...The harvest is so great, and the workers are so few. So pray to the one in charge of the harvesting, and ask him to recruit more workers for his harvest fields.

Jesus cures a very sick girl here, but the major point here is the need for more people to work for the Self instead of only the ego, as it were.

Matthew 10:2-4 (names of the Twelve): Simon (Peter), Andrew, James, John, Philip, Bartholomew, Thomas, Matthew (tax collector), James (2), Thaddaeus, Simon the Zealot, Judas.

FYI

Matthew 10:5-42 Don't go to the Gentiles or the Samaritans, but only to the people of Israel-God's lost sheep. Go and announce to them that the Kingdom of Heaven is near. Heal the sick, raise the dead, cure the lepers, and cast out demons. Give as freely as you have received! Don't take any money with you; don't even carry a duffle bag with extra clothes and shoes, or even a walking stick; for those you help should feed and care for you.

Whenever you enter a city or village, search for a godly man and stay in his home until you leave for the next town. When you ask permission to stay, be friendly, and if it turns out to be a godly home, give it your blessing; if not, keep the blessing. **Any city or home that doesn't welcome you-shake off the dust of that place from your feet as you leave.** Truly, the wicked cities of Sodom and Gomorrah will be better off at Judgment Day than they. I am sending you out as sheep among wolves. Be as wary as serpents and harmless as doves. But beware! For you will be arrested and tried, and whipped in the synagogues. Yes, and you must stand trial before governors and kings for my sake. This will give you the opportunity to tell them about me, yes, to witness to the world. When you are arrested, don't worry about what to say at your trial, for you will be given the right words at the right time. For it won't be you doing the talking-it will be the Spirit of your heavenly Father speaking through you! Brother shall betray brother to death, and fathers shall betray their own children. And children shall rise against their parents and cause their deaths. **Everyone shall hate you because you belong to me. But all of you who endure to the end shall be saved.** When you are persecuted in one city, flee to the next! I will return before you have reached them all! A student is not above his master. The student shares his teacher's fate. The servant shares his master's! And since I, the master of the household, have been called 'Satan,' how much more will you! But don't be afraid of those who threaten you. For the time is coming when the truth will be revealed: their secret plots will become public information. What I tell you now in the gloom, shout abroad when daybreak comes. What I whisper in your ears, proclaim from the housetops! Don't be afraid of those who can kill only your bodies-but can't touch your souls! Fear only God who can destroy both soul and body in hell. Not one sparrow (What do they cost? Two for a penny?) can fall to the ground without your Father knowing it. And the very hairs of your head are all numbered. So don't worry! You are more valuable to him than many sparrows. If anyone publicly acknowledges me as his friend, I will openly acknowledge him as my friend before my father in heaven. But if anyone publicly denies me, I will openly deny him before my Father in heaven. **Don't imagine that I came to bring peace to the earth! No, rather a sword.** I have come to set a man against his father, and a daughter against her mother, and a daughter-in-law against her mother-in-law- a man's worst enemies will be right in his own home! If you love your father and mother more than you love me, you are not worthy of being mine; or if you love your son or daughter more than me, you are not worthy of being mine. If you refuse to take up your cross and follow me, you are not worthy of being mine. If you cling to your life, you will lose it; but if you give it up for me, you will save it. Those who welcome you are welcoming me. And when they welcome me they are welcoming God who sent me. If you welcome a prophet because he is a man of God, you will be given the same reward a prophet gets. And if you welcome good and godly men because of their godliness, you will be given a reward like theirs. And if, as my representatives, you give even a cup of cold water to a little child, you will surely be rewarded.

Jesus does not want any baggage (what the ego wishes to hold on to, be it material things, our psychological attitudes/states, etc.) being carried in pursuit of doing the work of the Self.

Anyone who cannot and/or will not accept this message is not to be attacked but rather left to wallow in his or her current state pending a conscious attitude shift. The work of spreading such things can be dangerous (sheep among wolves), but we have to be careful about evangelization because individuation is unique to different people. Following the Self and doing the proper things in a given context is often an unpopular undertaking, and it may create misery in the moment. But whoever sees the process through to the end will be saved, gaining greater transformation and completeness. Since students/apprentices become like their teachers/masters, we are expected to live our lives according to the Self, just as Jesus did, and we will not be spared our crosses, as they are required for growth.

The statement by Jesus that he came to bring not peace, but a sword, is psychologically critical. Only through the conflict and clash of opposites can development and transformation take place. No one changes when things are going well or in the absence of tension. The Self demands that it be primary, which is why Jesus says what he says following the peace/sword statement.

Matthew 11:4-30 Go back to John and tell him about the miracles you've seen me do-the blind people I've healed, and the lame people now walking without help, and the cured lepers, and the deaf who hear, and the dead raised to life; and tell him about my preaching the Good News to the poor. Then give him this message, 'Blessed are those who don't doubt me...' When you went out into the barren wilderness to see John, what did you expect him to be like? Grass blowing in the wind? Or were you expecting to see a man dressed as a prince in a palace?

Or a prophet of God? Yes, and he is more than just a prophet. For John is the man mentioned in the Scriptures-a messenger to precede me, to announce my coming, and prepare people to receive me. Truly, of all men ever born, none shines more brightly than John the Baptist. And yet, even the lesser lights in the Kingdom of Heaven will be greater than he is! And from the time John the Baptist began preaching and baptizing until now, ardent multitudes have been crowding toward the Kingdom of Heaven, for all the laws and prophets looked forward [to the Messiah]. Then John appeared, and if you are willing to understand what I mean, he is Elijah, the one the prophets said would come [at the time the Kingdom begins]. If ever you were willing to listen, listen now! What shall I say about this nation? These people are like children playing, who say to their little friends, 'We played wedding and you weren't happy, so we played funeral but you weren't sad.' For John the Baptist doesn't even drink wine and often goes without food, and you say, 'He's crazy.' And I, the Messiah, feast and drink, and you complain that I am 'a glutton and a drinking man, and hang around with the worst sort of sinners!' But brilliant men like you can justify your every inconsistency!...Woe to you, Chorazin, and woe to you, Bethsaida! For if the miracles I did in your streets had been done in wicked Tyre and Sidon their people would have repented long ago in shame and humility. Truly, Tyre and Sidon will be better off on the Judgment Day than you! And Capernaum, though highly honored, shall go down to hell! For if the marvelous miracles I did in you had been done in Sodom, it would still be here today. Truly, Sodom will be better off at the Judgment Day than you...O Father, Lord of heaven and earth, thank you for hiding the truth from those who think themselves so wise, and for revealing it to little children. Yes, Father, for it pleased you to do it this way! Everything has been entrusted to me by my Father. Only the Father knows the Son, and the Father is known only by the Son **and by those to whom the Son reveals him.** Come to me and I will give you rest-all of you who work so hard beneath a heavy yoke. Wear my yoke-for it fits perfectly-and let me teach you, for I am gentle and humble, and you shall find rest for your souls; for I give you only light burdens.

Anyone who is a champion for the Self will be praised, as Jesus does here with John the Baptist. And so often those who signal something important appear lowly, as John did. When we reject what isn't appealing, it can create a *Beauty and the Beast* situation when the prince rejects the ugly woman and is turned into the Beast as a result. We have to answer the door and be welcoming, just like Philemon and Baucis did/were in the Greek tradition. The truth is indeed often hidden from those who think they have it but revealed to those with a childlike attitude of openness and receptivity as well as that teleological/future-oriented symbolism that children have, things that allow for opposites to be unified and transcended into higher completeness.

Please take note of Jesus saying that God may be revealed to people. This fact must be thought about before deeming someone "crazy," like John the Baptist and so many others have been, both ordinary and extraordinary people alike. Following the Self usually does not result in light burdens from an empirical standpoint, certainly not initially, and this is another area where Jesus appears to contradict himself, but he is referring to the presence of the light side of the Self, which does indeed bring rest and peace.

Matthew 12:3-13 Haven't you ever read what King David did when he and his friends were hungry? He went into the Temple and they ate the special bread permitted to the priests alone. That was breaking the law too. And haven't you ever read in the law of Moses how the priests on duty in the Temple may work on the Sabbath? And truly, one is here who is greater than the Temple! But if you had known the meaning of this Scripture verse, 'I want you to be merciful more than I want your offerings,' you would not have condemned those who aren't guilty! For I, the Messiah, am master even of the Sabbath...If you had just one sheep, and it fell into a well on the Sabbath, would you work to rescue it that day? Of course you would. And how much more valuable is a person than a sheep! Yes, it is right to do good on the Sabbath. Stretch out your arm. (heals)

We have seen this attitude from Jesus previously and will see it again…

Matthew 12:25-50 A divided kingdom ends in ruin. A city or home divided against itself cannot stand. And if Satan is casting out Satan, he is fighting himself, and destroying his own kingdom. And if, as you claim, I am casting out demons by invoking the powers of Satan, then what power do your own people use when they cast them out? Let them answer your accusation! But if I am casting out demons by the Spirit of God, then the Kingdom of God has arrived among you. One cannot rob Satan's kingdom without first binding Satan. Only then can his demons be cast out! Anyone who isn't helping me is harming me. Even blasphemy against me or any other sin can be forgiven-all except one speaking against the Holy Spirit shall never be forgiven, either in this world or in the world to come. A tree is identified by its fruit. A tree from a select variety produces good fruit; poor varieties don't. You brood of snakes! How could evil men like you speak what is good and right? For a man's heart determines his speech. A good man's speech reveals the rich treasures within him. An evil-hearted man is filled with venom, and his speech reveals it. And I tell you this, that you must give account on Judgment Day for very idle word you speak. Your words now reflect your fate then: either you will be justified by them or you will be condemned...Only an evil, faithless generation would ask for further proof; and none will be given except what happened to Jonah the prophet! For as Jonah was in the great fish for three days and three nights, so I, the Messiah, shall be in the heart of the earth three days and three nights. The men of Nineveh shall arise against this nation at the judgment and condemn you. For when Jonah preached to them, they repented and turned to God from all their evil ways. And now a greater than Jonah is here-and you refuse to believe him. The Queen of Sheba shall rise against this nation in the judgment, and condemn it; for she came from a distant land to hear the wisdom of Solomon; and now a greater than Solomon is here-and you refuse to believe him. This evil nation is like a man possessed by a demon. For if the demon leaves, it goes into the deserts for a while, seeking rest but finding none. Then it says, 'I will return to the man I came from.' So it returns and finds the man's heart clean but empty! Then the demon finds seven other spirits more evil than itself, and all enter the man and live in him. And so he is worse off than before...Who is my mother? Who are my brothers? Look! These are my mother and brothers. Anyone who obeys my Father in heaven is my brother, sister, and mother!

Here we have the famous statement from Jesus that a divided house cannot stand. This "house" could be a country, the whole earth, a family, or, most importantly, us. What that means psychologically is that *everything*, light and dark, must be integrated and transformed. We must become *whole/complete* to the greatest extent possible via the union and transcendence of opposites. The issue of blasphemy against the Holy Spirit was discussed in Mark's Gospel, and we are aware that we have to judge by fruits/actions, not by words or appearances.

However, this idea about Satan fighting himself and destroying his kingdom is true, meaning it must also be true of God as well. Job and others force God to become aware of that uncomfortable fact, and to split the divine into Jesus and Satan is a breaking apart of opposites instead of integrating them in a *whole* instead of a partial God. Now we can see why Meister Eckhart and others prayed for God to help them against God[50]. Full elaboration of this area has to wait for John's Gospel because it most clearly points in this direction among the four Gospels.

Jesus also notes the night-sea journey of Jonah and his own time at the hands of death, and this parallels empirical experience from every psychotherapy patient and people in general. The surrender-journey/endurance-transformation progression is how any significant shifts occur from a psychological standpoint.

---

50. see J. Dourley - On Behalf of the Mystical Fool: Jung on the Religious Situation

Many of Edinger's works talk about the psychology of the Queen of Sheba, and the reader can check the references section for many of his books. She is important for bringing the feminine into focus, which is a shadow area of all three major organized Western religions (Christianity, Islam, and Judaism). Finally, Jesus is impeccably correct about more demons (shadow areas/complexes) appearing when one "leaves," and only following the directives of the Self and embracing one's whole personality can the cycle of relapse be prevented. Those who work towards this development and transformation are indeed Jesus' family, as he states.

Matthew 13:3-23 (parable of the Sower) A farmer was sowing grain in his fields. As he scattered the seed across the ground, some fell beside a path, and the birds came and ate it. And some fell on rocky soil where there was little depth of earth; the plants sprang up quickly enough in the shallow soil, but the hot sun soon scorched them and they withered and died, for they had so little root. Other seeds fell among thorns, and the thorns choked out the tender blades. But some fell on good soil, and produced a crop that was thirty, sixty, and even a hundred times as much as he had planted. If you have ears, listen!...For to him who has will more be given, and he will have great plenty; but from him who has not, even the little he has will be taken away. **That is why I use these illustrations, so people will hear and see but not understand**. This fulfills the prophecy of Isaiah: 'They hear, but don't understand; they look, but don't see! For their hearts are fat and heavy, and their ears are dull, and they have closed their eyes in sleep, so they won't see and hear and understand and turn to God again, and let me heal them.' But blessed are your eyes, for they see; and your ears, for they hear. Many a prophet and godly man has longed to see what you have seen, and hear what you have heard, but couldn't. Now here is an explanation of the story I told about the farmer planting grain: The hard path where some of the seeds fell represents the heart of a person who hears the Good News about the Kingdom and doesn't understand it; then Satan comes and snatches away the seeds from his heart. The shallow, rocky soil represents the heart of a man who hears the message and receives it with real joy, but he doesn't have much depth in his life, and the seeds don't root very deeply, and after a while when trouble comes, or persecution begins because of his beliefs, his enthusiasm fades, and he drops out. The ground covered with thistles represents a man who hears the message, but the cares of this life and his longing for money choke out God's Word, and he does less and less for God. The good ground represents the heart of a man who listens to the message and understands it and goes out and brings thirty, sixty, or even a hundred others into the Kingdom.

Jesus explains this critical parable of the Sower, and the seed is the Good News. However, do people get to choose what type of ground they are, as it were? The answer is certainly not if sufficient conscious awareness is not present, and some people really are dealt a hand, via medical/psychological or environmental circumstances, for example, that simply cannot be played to a substantial extent, if really at all. This isn't an excuse to quit trying, but it is empirical reality. Just look around you and pay attention; have eyes to see and ears to hear! But Jesus speaks in parables/riddles because he is aware that some people are not yet ready to accept the full meaning.

Once conscious awareness reaches a critical level, the meaning emerges in direct proportion to the awareness. This creates transformation in ourselves, which in turn brings along others, as Jesus notes.

Matthew 13:24-30 The Kingdom of Heaven is like a farmer sowing good seed in his field; but one night as he slept, his enemy came and sowed thistles among the wheat. When the crop began to grow; the thistles grew too. The farmer's men came and told him, 'Sir, the field where you planted that choice seed is full of thistles!' 'An enemy has done it,' he exclaimed. 'Shall we pull out the thistles?' they asked. 'No,' he replied. 'You'll hurt the wheat if you do. Let both grow together until the harvest, and I will tell the reapers to sort out the thistles and burn them, and put the wheat in the barn.'

In other words, the light and the dark will coexist here in the space-time frame. Eventually a day of reckoning arrives where development and transformation must be chosen/otherwise rule the day, but that involves awareness and integration of the opposites within us. Jesus knew this, and "burning the thistles" is more about accepting and transforming our shadow areas and complexes than eliminating things humans define as "bad." Trying to get rid of these parts of ourselves would indeed kill or harm the "wheat," as there would be no opportunity for the type of evolution described here.

Matthew 13:31-32 The Kingdom of Heaven is like a tiny mustard seed planted in a field. It is the smallest of all seeds, but becomes the largest of all plants, and grows into a tree where birds can come and find shelter.

See analysis in Mark's Gospel; even a tiny amount of energy can be multiplied, just not zero.

Matthew 13:33 The Kingdom of Heaven can be compared to a woman making bread. She takes a measure of flour and mixes in the yeast until it permeates every part of the dough.

The yeast is the Self, which Jesus symbolizes, and the way the process is described here is exactly the way the Force in Star Wars is presented: it is pervasive everywhere and in everything. The Force and the Holy Spirit have much in common.

Matthew 13:37-57 All right, I am the farmer who sows the choice seed. The field is the world, and the seed represents the people of the Kingdom; the thistles are the people belonging to Satan. The enemy who sowed the thistles among the wheat is the devil; the harvest is the end of the world, and the reapers are the angels. Just as in this story the thistles are separated and burned, so shall it be at the end of the world. I will send my angels and they will separate out of the Kingdom every temptation and all who are evil, and throw them into the furnace and burn them. There shall be weeping and gnashing of teeth. Then the godly shall shine as the sun in their Father's Kingdom. Let those with ears, listen! The Kingdom of Heaven is like a treasure a man discovered in a field. In his excitement, he sold everything he owned to get enough money to buy the field-and get the treasure, too! Again, the Kingdom of Heaven is like a pearl merchant on the lookout for choice pearls. He discovered a real bargain-a pearl of great value-and sold everything he owned to purchase it! Again, the Kingdom of Heaven can be illustrated by a fisherman-he casts a net into the water and gathers in fish off every kind, valuable and worthless. When the net is full, he drags it up onto the beach and sits down and sorts out the edible ones into crates and throws the others away. That is the way it will be at the end of the world-the angels will come and separate the wicked people from the godly, casting the wicked into the fire; there shall be weeping and gnashing of teeth. Do you understand?...These experts in Jewish law who are now my disciples have double treasures-from the Old Testament as well as from the New!...A prophet is honored everywhere except in his own country, and among his own people!

Jesus gets apocalyptic/eschatological about the lessons here, but again we have to keep the above points about integration of shadows and complexes in mind and remember the audience to whom he was speaking (very black and white perception of gray reality at that time) as well as the problem with human definitions of good and evil. This is in part why Jesus will shortly tell Peter to "get behind him, Satan" and quit thinking as humans do. Prophets are never recognized among their own (just try to tell a sibling what to do, for example!), and dropping everything anti-transformational one is doing is required to achieve that proverbial treasure or pearl of great price, which is connection to the Cosmic Self (God).

Matthew 14:16-31 (loaves and fishes) That isn't necessary-you feed them!...Bring them here...Don't be afraid! (Jesus walking on water)....All right, come along (to Peter)...O man of little faith. Why did you doubt me?

See Mark's Gospel for analysis of the loaves and fishes episode. Water is often a symbol of the unconscious, so of course the Self asks us to go there for development and transformation.

Matthew 15:3-20 And why do your traditions violate the direct commandments of God? For instance, God's law is 'Honor your father and mother; anyone who reviles his parents must die. But you say, 'Even if your parents are in need, you may give their support money to the church instead.' And so, by your man-made rule, you nullify the direct command of God to honor and care for your parents. You hypocrites! Well did Isaiah prophesy of you, 'These people say they honor me, but their hearts are far away. Their worship is worthless, for they teach their man-made laws instead of those from God.' Listen to what I say and try to understand. You aren't made unholy by eating non-kosher food! It is what you *say* and *think* that makes you unclean...Every plant not planted by my Father shall be rooted up, so ignore them. They are blind guides leading the blind, and both will fall into a ditch...Don't you understand? Don't you see that anything you eat passes through the digestive tract and out again? But evil words come from an evil heart, and defile the man who says them. For from the heart come evil thoughts, murder, adultery, fornication, theft, lying, and slander. These are what defile; but there is no spiritual defilement from eating without first going through the ritual of ceremonial handwashing!

Three big points by Jesus here: the directives of the Self supersede the laws of the ego, what is in our hearts is what matters most, and the blind (unaware) cannot lead the blind, for they all will indeed fall into a ditch.

Matthew 15:24-28 I was sent to help the Jews-the lost sheep of Israel-not the Gentiles...It doesn't seem right to take bread from the children and throw it to the dogs...Woman, your faith is large, and your request is granted.

This well-known Gospel episode shows two things. Jesus (the Self) is for everyone, and persistence in a righteous and faithful way can have an effect on God, as is illustrated here.

Matthew 15:32-34 I pity these people-they've been here with me for three days now, and have nothing left to eat; I don't want to send them away hungry or they will faint along the road...How much food do you have? (Jesus feeds 4,000)

Same analysis as the loaves and fishes episode.

Matthew 16:2-4 You are good at reading the weather signs of the skies-red sky tonight means fair weather tomorrow; red sky in the morning means foul weather all day-but you can't read the obvious signs of the times! **This evil, unbelieving nation is asking for some strange sign in the heavens, but no further proof will be given except the miracle that happened to Jonah.**

This is a monumentally critical passage that evil (functioning away from development and transformation as directed by the Self) and unaware/unfaithful people are not going to receive signs or miracles, but only the sign of Jonah, which is surrender-insight/endurance-transformation[51]. That progression creates the true miracle.

Matthew 16:6-11 Watch out! Beware of the yeast of the Pharisees and Sadducees...O men of little faith! Why are you so worried about having no food? Won't you ever understand? Don't you remember at all the 5,000 I fed with five loaves, and the basketfuls left over? Don't you remember the 4,000 I fed,

---

51. One cannot escape the swamp, as it were. See J. Hollis – Swamplands of the Soul: New Life in Dismal Places.

and all that was left? How could you even think I was talking about food? But again I say, 'Beware of the yeast of the Pharisees and Sadducees.' (their wrong teaching)

Yeast is a concept used in various ways by Jesus, and here, like any archetypal entity taking on the character of the context (archetypes contain the opposites and are generally neutral; the conscious attitude determines how they function), it manifests in a negative way due to the interaction with the Pharisees and Sadducees. Again, clergy of *any* organized religion, take note!

Matthew 16:13-19 Who are the people saying I am?...Who do *you* think I am?...God has blessed you, Simon, son of Jonah, for my Father in heaven has personally revealed this to you-this is not from any human source. **You are Peter, a stone; and upon this rock I will build my church; and all the powers of hell shall not prevail against it.** And I will give you the keys of the Kingdom of Heaven; whatever doors you lock on earth shall be locked in heaven; and whatever doors you open on earth shall be open in heaven!

Jesus noted in the parable of the Sower how we affect everyone and everything around us by our conscious attitude towards our whole being and its implementation, and that is the meaning of having the keys to the Kingdom. Again, the observer affects the observed, which is why becoming more objective about our own subjectivity is so important. He chooses to build his church (the community of believers – us) with Peter as the rock, but nowhere does he say that rock is perfect or correct all the time. Out the window goes the Catholic papal infallibility idea some believe. Our true rock is always the Self, of which Jesus is the symbol for Christians.

Matthew 16:23-28 (Peter says Jesus will not die) **Get away from me, you Satan! You are a dangerous trap to me. You are thinking merely from a human point of view, and not from God's. If anyone wants to be a follower of mine, let him deny himself and take up his cross and follow me. For anyone who keeps his life for himself shall lose it; and anyone who loses his life for me shall find it again.** What profit is there if you gain the whole world-and lose eternal life? What can be compared with the value of eternal life? For I, the Son of Mankind, shall come with my angels in the glory of my Father and judge each person according to his deeds. And some of you standing right here now will certainly live to see me coming in my Kingdom.

Here is the admonition by Jesus to Peter to get behind him, Satan. Jesus knows he must die and rise, but Peter, thinking like humans do (shallowly), doesn't get it. The will of the ego must be sacrificed for the sake of the Self. We must lose our lives to find them on a new level, and we must unlearn what we have learned to become more aware. Some will accomplish this to a greater or lesser extent and see the Self manifest in fullness (Jesus coming in his Kingdom). If Jesus expected Peter, a simple fisherman with a 2,000 year old mindset, to understand, then he certainly expects us to get the point.

Matthew 17:1-7 (Transfiguration of Jesus) – Get up. Don't be afraid.

Any such direct experience of the divine, archetypal psyche will create fear, regardless of whether it is positive or negative. This is why Jesus, angels, etc. often begin with "be not afraid" when appearing, because such an event will be overwhelming to the psyche.

**Matthew 17:11-12** They are right. Elijah must come and set everything in order. And, in fact, he has already come, but he wasn't recognized, and was badly mistreated by many. And I, the Messiah, shall also suffer at their hands. (speaking of John the Baptist)

How true, as we have already seen!

**Matthew 17:17-27** Oh, you stubborn, faithless people! How long shall I bear with you? Bring him here to me (casts out demon disciples couldn't and they wonder why)...Because of your little faith. For if you had faith even as small as a tiny mustard seed you could say to this mountain, 'Move!' and it would go far away. Nothing would be impossible. But this kind of demon won't leave unless you have prayed and gone without food...I am going to be betrayed into the power of those who will kill me, and on the third day afterwards I will be brought back to life again...What do you think, Peter? Do kings levy assessments against their own people, or against conquered foreigners?...Well, then, the citizens are free! However, we don't want to offend them, so go down to the shore and throw in a line, and open the mouth of the first fish you catch. You will find a coin to cover the taxes for both of us; take it and pay them.

Jesus again gets a bit frustrated with the faithlessness and ignorance of the disciples, but this passage suggests that some demons (usually psychological issues in today's terms) do require divine intervention of some sort. And again, we see the idea of paying Caesar what is Caesar's as previously discussed. As for being free, personally that depends on the level and implementation of conscious awareness, and as a society on the government to quit its quest for power and control.

Matthew 18:2-35 Unless you turn to God from your sins and become as little children, you will never get into the Kingdom of Heaven. Therefore anyone who humbles himself as this little child, is the greatest in the Kingdom of Heaven. And any of you who welcomes a little child like this because you are mine, is welcoming me and caring for me. But if any of you causes one of these little ones who trusts in me to lose his faith, it would be better for you to have a rock tied to your neck and be thrown into the sea. Woe upon the world for all its evils. Temptation to do wrong is inevitable, but woe to the man who does the tempting. So if your hand or foot causes you to sin, cut it off and throw it away. Better to enter heaven crippled than to be in hell with both of your hands and feet. And if your eye causes you to sin, gouge it out and throw it away. Better to enter heaven with one eye than to be in hell with two. Beware that you don't look down upon a single one of these little children. For I tell you that in heaven their angels have constant access to my Father. And I, the Messiah, came to save the lost. If a man has a hundred sheep, and one wanders away and is lost, what will he do? Won't he leave the ninety-nine others and go out into the hills to search for the lost one? And if he finds it, he will rejoice over it more than over thee ninety-nine others safe at home! Just so, it is not my Father's will that even one of these little ones should perish. If a brother sins against you, go to him privately and confront him with his fault. If he listens and confesses it, you have won back a brother. But if not, then take one or two others with you and go back to him again, proving everything you say by these witnesses. If he still refuses to listen, then take your case to the church, and if the church's verdict favors you, but he won't accept it, then the church should excommunicate him. And I tell you this-whatever you bind on earth is bound in heaven, and whatever you free on earth will be freed in heaven. I also tell you this-if two of you agree down here on earth concerning anything you ask for, my Father in heaven will do it for you. For where two or three gather together because they are mine, I will be right there among them...No! Seventy times seven! The Kingdom of Heaven can be compared to a king who decided to bring his accounts up to date. In the process, one of his debtors was brought in who owed him $10,000,000! He couldn't pay, so the king ordered him sold for the debt, also his wife and children and everything he had. But the man fell down before the king, his face in the dust, and said, 'Oh, sir, be patient with me and I will pay it all.' Then the king was filled with pity for him and released him and forgave his debt. But when the man left the king, he went to a man who owed him $2,000 and grabbed him by the throat and demanded instant payment. The man fell down before him and begged him to give him a little time. 'Be patient and I will pay it,' he pled. But his creditor wouldn't wait. He had the man arrested and jailed until thee debt would be paid in full. Then the man's friends went to the king and told him what had happened. And the king called before him the man he had forgiven and said, 'you evil-hearted wretch! Here I forgave you all that tremendous debt, just because you asked me to-shouldn't you have mercy on others, just as I had mercy on you? Then the angry king sent the man to the torture chamber until he had paid every last penny due. So shall my heavenly Father do to you if you refuse to truly forgive your brothers.

Here is a repeat of the childlike, individuation-oriented attitude required to achieve a state of Heaven, Nirvana, etc. The idea of cutting away body parts causing sin is of course not literal, but refers to pruning away and/or integrating material connected to shadow (underdeveloped) areas and complexes, as these can block development and transformation and are therefore "sinful." Saving the lost is what the Self aims to do, and energy does tend to go towards those struggling the most. There is a two-way benefit to that, both for the people and the Self.

Jesus also discusses how to handle disputes by the proper channels here; it's pretty direct and self-explanatory, and we can understand the excommunication comment as another way of making his previous statement about shaking the dust off your feet and moving on. The comment about God being present where several people gather and ask for something is complicated with all the suffering and disasters happening constantly around us, but God is in fact there (omnipresent). The issue is what is being asked for may be ego-based instead of Self-based and/or the aspect(s) of God that are involved in that context. This will make more sense, again, when we reach John's Gospel, but God, to the extent that we can observe from our limited perspective, does answer prayers, as it were, just often not how we think God should! Finally, as illustrated by the story here, if we fail to show mercy and forgiveness, it will not be shown to us. The observer affects the observed, and nature shows us the face we show it.

Matthew 19:4-12 Don't you read the Scriptures? In them it is written that at the beginning God created man and woman, and that a man should leave his father and mother, and be forever united to his wife. The two shall become one-no longer two, but one! And no man may divorce what God has joined together... Moses did that in recognition of your hard and evil hearts, but it was not what God had originally intended. And I tell you this, that anyone who divorces his wife, except for fornication, and marries another, commits adultery...Not everyone can accept this statement. Only those whom God helps. Some are born without the ability to marry, and some are disabled by men, and some refuse to marry for the sake of the Kingdom of Heaven. Let anyone who can, accept my statement.

This marriage/union of opposites comment was discussed previously, but Jesus additionally notes that connection to the Self is required for proper functioning and that different people are called to individuation by many paths.

Matthew 19:14 Let the little children come to me, and don't prevent them. For such is the Kingdom of Heaven.

See Mark's Gospel for the important meaning here.

Matthew 19:17-30 When you call me good you are calling me God, for God alone is truly good. But to answer your question, you can get to heaven if you keep the commandments...Don't kill, don't commit adultery, don't steal, don't lie, honor your father and mother, and love your neighbor as yourself!...If you want to be perfect, go and sell everything you have and give the money to the poor, and you will have treasure in heaven; and come, follow me...**It is almost impossible for a rich man to get into the Kingdom of Heaven.** I say it again-it is easier for a camel to go through the eye of a needle than for a rich man to enter the Kingdom of God!...Humanly speaking, no one. But with God, everything is possible...When I, the Messiah, shall sit upon my glorious throne in the Kingdom, you my disciples shall certainly sit on twelve thrones judging the twelve tribes of Israel. And anyone who gives up his home, brothers, sisters, father, mother, wife, children, or property, to follow me, shall receive a hundred times as much in return, and shall have eternal life. But many who are last now will be first then.

Here is an amalgamation of ideas we have already discussed, but as a reminder, the Self must always be primary compared to the ego (or anything else). The emptying process (Greek: *kenosis*) is very important here.

Matthew 20:1-16 The owner of an estate went out early one morning to hire workers for his harvest field. He agreed to pay them $20 a day and sent them out to work. A couple of hours later he was passing a hiring hall and saw some men standing around waiting for jobs, so he sent them also into his fields, telling them he would pay them whatever was right at the end of the day. At noon and again around three o'clock in the afternoon he did the same thing. At 5 o'clock that evening he was in town again and saw some more men standing around and asked them, 'Why haven't you been working today?' 'Because no one hired us,' they replied. 'Then go on out and join the others in my fields,' he told them. That evening he told the paymaster to call the men in and pay them, beginning with the last men first. When the men hired at 5 o'clock were paid, each received $20. So when the men hired earlier came to get theirs, they assumed they would receive much more. But they, too, were paid $20. They protested, 'Those fellows worked only one hour, and yet you've paid them just as much as those of us who worked all day, in the scorching heat.' 'Friend,' he answered one of them, 'I did you no wrong!' Didn't you agree to work all day for $20? Take it and go. It is my desire to pay all the same; is it against the law to give away my money if I want to? Should you be angry because I am kind? And so it is that the last shall be first, and the first, last.

This is an illustration of the Kingdom of Heaven, and it actually is not socialist though it appears to be on the surface. Aside from the obvious implications about honoring contracts, and on the other end, fair pay, the point here is that any work done towards the Kingdom (i.e. the Cosmic Self) is valuable to every entity involved, and it shows yet again that God is less concerned about what has been done, though he certainly cares as Jesus notes many times regarding following laws, than development and transformation. The point is doing the work in the field, and it may be that the last to arrive did the most transformation; we aren't privy to what others are doing internally or even externally. But if you do the psychological work in service of the Self/God, you will be paid. Everyone in the field did work and got rewarded, and the griping is coming from a human standpoint, for which Peter was already rebuked by Jesus. Here, such comparisons are largely irrelevant in the grand scheme of things.

Matthew 20:18-33 I will be betrayed to the chief priests and other Jewish leaders, and they will hand me over to the Roman government, and I will be mocked and crucified, and the third day I will rise to life again...What is your request?...You don't know what you are asking!...Are you able to drink from the terrible cup I am about to drink from?...You shall indeed drink from it. But I have no right to say who will sit on the thrones next to mine. Those places are reserved for the persons my Father selects...Among the heathen, kings are tyrants and each minor official lords it over those beneath him. But among you it is quite different. Anyone wanting to be a leader among you must be your servant. And if you want to be right at the top, you must serve like a slave. **Your attitude must be like my own, for I, the Messiah, did not come to be served, but to serve, and to give my life as a ransom for many**...What do you want me to do for you? (heals blind people)

Again, a few ideas we have already discussed, and I would again emphasize that we are expected to carry our crosses for the sake of development and transformation, just as Jesus did.

Matthew 21:2-27 Just as you enter, you will see a donkey tied there, with its colt beside it. Untie them and bring them here. If anyone asks you what you are doing, just say, 'The Master needs them,' and there will be no trouble...The Scriptures say my Temple is a place of prayer, but you have turned it into a den of thieves (overturns tables in the Temple)...Yes. Didn't you ever read the Scriptures? For they say, 'Even little babies shall praise him!'... (to fig tree) Never bear fruit again!...Truly, if you have faith, and don't doubt, you can do things like this and much more. You can even say to this Mount of Olives, 'Move over into the ocean,' and it will. You can get anything-*anything* you ask for in prayer-if you believe...I'll tell you if you answer one question first. Was John the Baptist sent from God, or not? (they won't answer)...Then I won't answer your question either.

All of these episodes were addressed in our analysis of Mark's Gospel...

Matthew 21:28-44 But what do you think about this? A man with two sons told the older boy, 'Son, go out and work on the farm today.' 'I won't,' he answered, but later he changed his mind and went. Then the father told the youngest, 'You go!' and he said, 'Yes, sir, I will.' But he didn't. Which of the two was obeying his father?...Surely evil men and prostitutes will get into the Kingdom before you do. For John the Baptist told you to repent and turn to God, and you wouldn't, while very evil men and prostitutes did. And even when you saw this happening, you refused to repent, and so you couldn't believe. Now listen to this story: A certain landowner planted a vineyard with a hedge around it, and built a platform for the watchman, then leased the vineyard to some farmers on a sharecrop basis, and went away to live in another country. At the time of the grape harvest he sent his agents to the farmers to collect his share. But the farmers attacked his men, beat one, killed one, and stoned another. Then he sent a larger group of his men to collect for him, but the results were the same. Finally the owner sent his son, thinking they would surely respect him. But when these farmers saw the son coming they said among themselves, 'Here comes the heir to this estate; come on, let's kill him and get it for ourselves!' So they dragged him out of the vineyard and killed him. When the owner returns, what do you think he will do to those farmers?...Didn't you ever read in the Scriptures: **'The stone rejected by the builders has been made the honored cornerstone, how remarkable! What an amazing thing the Lord has done'**? What I mean is that the Kingdom of God shall be taken away from you, and given to a nation that will give God his share of the crop. All who stumble on this rock of truth shall be broken, but those it falls on will be scattered as dust.

The beginning of this section shows that actions speak louder than words, and we again have an iteration of the landowner story already discussed. The stone that the builders rejected is an exact description of the Philosopher's stone in alchemy, and it is the true gold that must be sought above all else. Maintaining a healthy connection to the Self via the ego-Self axis is the way to keep developing and transforming while getting closer to individuation and the Kingdom.

Matthew 22:1-14 For instance, it can be illustrated by the story of a king who prepared a great wedding dinner for his son. Many guests were invited, and when the banquet was ready he sent messengers to notify everyone that it was time to come. But all refused! So he sent other servants to tell them, 'Everything is ready and the roast is in the oven. Hurry!' But the guests he had invited merely laughed and went on about their business, one to his farm, another to his store; others beat up his messengers and treated them shamefully, even killing some of them. Then the angry king sent out his army and destroyed the murderers and burned their city. And he said to his servants, 'The wedding feast is ready, and the guests I invited aren't worthy of the honor. Now go out to the street corners and invite everyone you see.' So the servants did, and brought in all they could find, good and bad alike; and the banquet hall was filled with guests. But when the king came in to meet the guests he noticed a man who wasn't wearing the wedding robe [provided for him]. 'Friend,' he asked, 'how does it happen that you are here without a wedding robe?' And the man had no reply. Then the king said to his aides, 'Bind him hand and foot and throw him out into the outer darkness where there is weeping and gnashing of teeth. For many are called, but few are chosen.'

This wedding feast parable illustrates that the Kingdom is ultimately open to all who accept it and show up ready for it (unlike the man not wearing the proper garments). The Self doesn't react well to being ignored or dismissed, but everyone is called. However, few are able to develop the required conscious attitude (hard) and put it into action (harder), and that's what Jesus means when he says few are chosen.

Matthew 22:18-46 You hypocrites! Who are you trying to fool with your trick questions? Here, show me a coin...Whose picture is stamped on it? And whose name is this beneath the picture?... **Well, then, give it to Caesar if it is his, and give God everything that belongs to God**...Your error is caused by your ignorance of the Scriptures and of God's power! For in the resurrection there is no marriage; everyone is as the angels in heaven. But now, as to whether there is a resurrection of the dead-don't you ever read the Scriptures? Don't you realize that God was speaking directly to you when he said, 'I *am* the God of Abraham, Isaac, and Jacob?' So God is not the God of the dead, but of the *living*...'**Love the Lord your God with all your heart, soul, and mind.' This is the first and greatest commandment. The second most important is similar: 'Love your neighbor as much as you love yourself.' All the other commandments and all the demands of the prophets stem from these two laws and are fulfilled if you obey them.** Keep only these and you will find that you are obeying all the others...What about the Messiah? Whose son is he? (reply is David's) Then why does David, speaking under the inspiration of the Holy Spirit, call him 'Lord?' For David said, 'God said to my Lord, sit at my right hand until I put your enemies beneath your feet.' Since David called him 'Lord,' how can he be merely his son?

This is important information that was discussed in context of Mark's Gospel.

Matthew 23:2-39 You would think these Jewish leaders and these Pharisees were Moses, the way they keep making up so many laws! And of course you should obey their every whim! It may be all right to do what they say, but above anything else, *don't follow their example.* For they don't do what they tell you to do. They load you with impossible demands that they themselves don't even try to keep. Everything they do is done for show. They act holy by wearing on their arms little prayer boxes with Scripture verses inside, and by lengthening the memorial images of their robes. And how they love to sit at the head table at banquets, and in the reserved pews in the synagogue! How they enjoy the deference paid them on the streets, and to be called 'Rabbi' and 'Master!' Don't ever let anyone call you that. For only God is your Rabbi and all of you are on the same level, as brothers. And don't address anyone here on earth as 'Father,' for only God in heaven should be addressed like that. And don't be called 'Master,' for only one is your master, even the Messiah. The more lowly your service to others, the greater you are. To be the greatest, be a servant. **But those who think themselves great shall be disappointed and humbled, and those who humble themselves shall be exalted.** Woe to you, Pharisees, and you other religious leaders. Hypocrites! For you won't let others enter the Kingdom of Heaven, and won't go in yourselves. And you pretend to be holy, with all your long, public prayers in the streets, while you are evicting widows from their homes. Hypocrites! Yes, woe upon you hypocrites. For you go to all lengths to make one convert, and then turn him into twice the son of hell you are yourselves. Blind guides! Woe upon you! For your rule is that to swear 'By God's Temple' means nothing-you can break that oath, but to swear 'By the gold in the Temple' is binding! Blind fools! Which is greater, the gold, or the Temple that sanctifies the gold? And you say that to take an oath 'By the altar' can be broken, but to swear 'By the gifts on the altar' is binding! Blind! For which is greater, the gift on the altar, or the altar itself that sanctifies the gift? When you swear 'By the altar' you are swearing by it and everything on it, and when you swear 'By the Temple' you are swearing by it, and by God who lives in it. And when you swear 'By heavens' you are swearing by the Throne of God and by God himself. Yes, woe upon you, Pharisees, and you other religious leaders-hypocrites! For you tithe down to the last mint leaf in your garden, but ignore the important things-justice and mercy and faith. Yes, you should tithe, but you shouldn't leave the more important things undone. Blind guides! You strain out a gnat and swallow a camel. Woe to you, Pharisees, and you religious leaders-hypocrites! You are so careful to polish the outside of the cup, but the inside is foul with extortion and greed. Blind Pharisees! First cleanse the inside of the cup, and then the whole cup will be clean. Woe to you, Pharisees, and you religious leaders! You are like beautiful mausoleums-full of dead men's bones, and of foulness and corruption. You try to look like saintly men, but underneath those pious robes of yours are hearts besmirched with every sort of hypocrisy and sin. Yes, woe to you, Pharisees, and you religious leaders-hypocrites! For you build monuments to the prophets killed by your fathers and lay flowers on the graves of the godly men they destroyed, and say, 'We certainly would never have acted as our fathers did.' In saying that, you are accusing yourselves of being the sons of wicked men. And you are following in their steps, filling up the full measure of their evil. Snakes! Sons of vipers! How shall you escape the judgment of hell? I will send you prophets, and wise men, and inspired writers, and you will kill some by crucifixion, and rip open the backs of others with whips in your synagogues, and hound them from city to city, so that you will become guilty of all the blood of murdered godly men from righteous Abel to Zechariah (son of Barachiah), slain by you in the Temple between the altar and the sanctuary. Yes, all the accumulated judgment of the centuries shall break upon the heads of this very generation. O Jerusalem, Jerusalem, the city that kills the prophets, and stones all those God sends to her! How often I have wanted to gather your children together as a hen gathers her chicks beneath her wings, but you wouldn't let me. And now your house is left to you, desolate. For I tell you this, you will never see me again until you are ready to welcome the one sent to you from God.

There are four important points here. One, the so-called leaders and experts say all the right things but do not practice what they preach. I think Jesus is quite clear about what he thinks of hypocrites here! Two, being humble is a virtue, and though it is paradoxical, it is the way to exaltation in the final analysis. Three, what is on the inside (true character) is far more important than anything on the outside for show, and what really matters must be prioritized. Four, the truth must be accepted and integrated to develop, transform, and individuate. Again, all religious clergy of any type who have eyes to see and ears to hear ought to do so!

Matthew 24:2-51 All these buildings will be knocked down, with not one stone left on top of another!...Don't let anyone fool you. For many will come claiming to be the Messiah, and will lead many astray. When you hear of wars beginning, this does not signal my return, these must come, but the end is not yet. The nations and kingdoms of the earth will rise against each other and there will be famines and earthquakes in many places. But all this will be only the beginning of the horrors to come. Then you will be tortured and killed and hated all over the world because you are mine, and many of you shall fall back into sin and betray and hate each other. And many false prophets will appear and lead many astray. Sin will be rampant everywhere and will cool the love of many. But those enduring to the end shall be saved. And the Good News about the Kingdom will be preached throughout the whole world, so that all nations will hear it, and then, finally, the end will come. So, when you see the horrible thing (told about by Daniel the prophet) standing in a holy place, then those in Judea must flee into the Judean hills. Those on their porches must not even go inside to pack before they flee. Those in the fields should not return to their homes for their clothes. And woe to pregnant women and to those with babies in those days. And pray that your flight will not be in winter, or on the Sabbath. For there will be persecution such as the world has never before seen in all its history, and will never see again. In fact, unless those days are shortened, all mankind will perish. But they will be shortened for the sake of God's chosen people. Then if anyone tells you, 'The Messiah has arrived at such and such a place, or has appeared here or there,' don't believe it. For false Christs shall arise, and false prophets, and will do wonderful miracles, so that if it were possible, even God's chosen ones would be deceived. See, I have warned you. So if someone tells you the Messiah has returned and is out in the desert, don't bother to go and look. Or, that he is hiding at a certain place, don't believe it! For as the lightning flashes across the sky from east to west, so shall my coming be, when I, the Messiah, return. And wherever the carcass is, there the vultures will gather. Immediately after the persecution of those days the sun will be darkened, and the moon will not give light, and the stars will seem to fall from the heavens, and the powers overshadowing the earth will be convulsed. And then at last the signal of my coming will appear in the heavens and there will be deep mourning all around the earth. And the nations of the world will see me arrive in the clouds of heaven, with power and great glory. And I shall send forth my angels with the sound of a mighty trumpet blast, and they shall gather my chosen ones from the farthest ends of the earth and heaven. Now learn a lesson from the fig tree. When her branch is tender and the leaves begin to sprout, you know that summer is almost here. Just so, when you see all these things beginning to happen, you can know that my return is near, even at the doors. Then at last this age will come to its close. Heaven and earth will disappear, but my words remain forever. But no one knows the date and hour when the end will be-not even the angels. No, nor even God's Son. Only the Father knows. The world will be at ease-banquets and parties and weddings-just as it was in Noah's time before the sudden coming of the flood; people wouldn't believe what was going to happen until the flood actually arrived and took them all away. So shall my coming be. Two men will be working together in the fields, and one will be taken, the other left. Two women will be going about their household tasks; one will be taken, the other left. So be prepared, for you don't know what day your Lord is coming. Just as a man can prevent trouble from thieves by keeping watch for them, so you can avoid trouble by always being ready for my unannounced return. Are you a wise and faithful servant of the Lord? Have I given you the task of managing my household, to feed my children day by day? Blessings on you if I return and find you faithfully doing your work. I will put such faithful ones in charge of everything I own! But if you are evil and say to yourself, 'My Lord won't be coming for a while,' and begin oppressing your fellow servants, partying and getting drunk, your Lord will arrive unannounced and unexpected, and severely whip you and send you off to the judgment of the hypocrites; there will be weeping and gnashing of teeth.

This is the corresponding apocalyptic/eschatological section of Matthew's Gospel with a bit more detail than what we already saw and discussed in Mark. Two key points/reminders are that we must endure and see through the individuation process as far as we possibly can and be prepared for the moments that the Self knocks on the proverbial door.

Matthew 25:1-30 The Kingdom of Heaven can be illustrated by the story of ten bridesmaids who took their lamps and went to meet the bridegroom. But only five of them were wise enough to fill their lamps with oil, while the other five were foolish and forgot. So, when the bridegroom was delayed, they lay down to rest until midnight, when they were roused by the shout, 'The bridegroom is coming! Come out and welcome him!' All the girls jumped up and trimmed their lamps. Then the five who hadn't any oil begged the others to share with them, for their lamps were going out. But the others replied, 'We haven't enough. Go instead to the shops and buy some for yourselves.' But while they were gone, the bridegroom came, and those who were ready went in with him to the marriage feast, and the door was locked. Later, when the other five returned, they stood outside, calling, 'Sir, open the door for us!' But he called back, 'Go away! It is too late!' So stay awake and be prepared, for you do not know the date or moment of my return. Again, the Kingdom of Heaven can be illustrated by the story of a man going into another country, who called together his servants and loaned them money to invest for him while he was gone. He gave $5,000 to one, $2000 to another, and $1,000 to the last-dividing it in proportion to their abilities-and then left on his trip. The man who received the $5,000 began immediately to buy and sell with it and soon earned another $5,000. The man with $2,000 went right to work, too, and earned another $2,000. But the man who received the $1,000 dug a hole in the ground and hid the money for safekeeping. After a long time their master returned from his trip and called them to him to account for his money. The man to whom he had entrusted the $5,000 brought him $10,000. His master praised him for good work. 'You have been faithful in handling this small amount,' he told him, 'so now I will give you many more responsibilities. Begin the joyous tasks I have assigned to you.' Next came the man who had received the $2,000, with the report. 'Sir, you gave me $2,000 to use, and I have doubled it.' 'Good work,' his master said. 'You are a good and faithful servant. You have been faithful over this small amount, so now I will give you much more.' Then the man with the $1,000 came and said, 'Sir, I knew you were a hard man, and I was afraid you would rob me of what I earned, so I hid your money in the earth and here it is!' But his master replied, 'Wicked man! Lazy slave! Since you knew I would demand your profit, you should at least have put my money into the bank so I could have some interest. Take the money from this man and give it to the man with the $10,000. For the man who uses well what he is given shall be given more, and he shall have abundance. But from the man who is unfaithful, even what little responsibility he has shall be taken from him. And throw the useless servant out into outer darkness: there shall be weeping and gnashing of teeth.'

Here we have the lamps parable and the talents parable. The lamps parable shows what not being (psychologically/spiritually) prepared will create, though in at least one version of the story, all ten women get saved[52]. The point of the talents parable is that any gift, ability, or resource we have must be put to work and multiplied. If we fail to do so, even what we have will be taken away and "given" to those with the proper conscious attitude and implementation of it.

Matthew 25:31-46 But when I, the Messiah, shall come in my glory, and all the angels with me, then I shall sit upon my throne of glory. And all the nations shall be gathered before me. And I will separate the people as a shepherd separates the sheep from the goats, and place the sheep at my right hand, and the goats at my left. Then I, the King, shall say to those at my right, 'Come, blessed of my Father, into the Kingdom prepared for you from the founding of the world. For I was hungry and you fed me; I was thirsty and you gave me water; I was a stranger and you invited me into your homes; naked and you clothed me; sick and in prison, and you visited me.' Then these righteous ones will

---

52.   see M-L. Von Franz – Aurora Consurgens

reply, 'Sir, when did we ever see you hungry and feed you? Or thirsty and give you anything to drink? Or a stranger, and help you? Or naked, and clothe you? When did we ever see you sick or in prison, and visit you?' And I, the King will tell them, 'When you did it to these my brothers you were doing it to me!' Then I will turn to those on my left and say, 'Away with you, you cursed ones, into the eternal fire prepared for the devil and his demons. For I was hungry and you wouldn't feed me: thirsty, and you wouldn't give me anything to drink; a stranger, and you refused me hospitality; naked, and you wouldn't clothe me; sick, and in prison, and you didn't visit me.' Then they will reply, 'Lord, when did we ever see you hungry or thirsty or a stranger or naked or sick or in prison, and not help you?' And I will answer, 'When you refused to help the least of these my brothers, you were refusing help to me.' And they shall go away into eternal punishment; but the righteous into everlasting life.

We must learn to observe God in everyone and everything around us, and if we can act properly in context of the Self, we are able to individuate and transcend the constraints of time and space.

Matthew 26:2-64 As you know, the Passover celebration begins in two days, and I shall be betrayed and crucified...Why are you criticizing her? For she has done a good thing to me. You will always have the poor among you, but you won't always have me. She has poured this perfume on me to prepare my body for burial. And she will always be remembered for this deed. The story of what she has done will be told throughout the whole world, wherever the Good News is preached....Go into the city and see Mr. So-and So, and tell him 'Our Master says, my time has come, and I will eat the Passover meal with my disciples at your house'...One of you will betray me...It is the one I served first. For I must die just as was prophesied, but woe to the man by whom I am betrayed. Far better for that one if he had never been born...Yes (directly to Judas that he was the one to betray Him)...Take it and eat it, for this is my body...Each one drink from it, for this is my blood, sealing the New Covenant. It is poured out to forgive the sins of multitudes. Mark my words-I will not drink this wine again until the day I drink it new with you in my Father's Kingdom...Tonight you will all desert me. For it is written in the Scriptures that God will smite the Shepherd, and the sheep of the flock will be scattered. But after I have been brought back to life again I will go to Galilee, and meet you there...(to Peter) The truth is that this very night, before the cock crows at dawn, you will deny me three times!...My soul is crushed with horror and sadness to the point of death...stay here...stay awake with me...My Father! If it is possible, let this cup be taken away from me. But I want your will, not mine...Peter, couldn't you even stay awake with me one hour? Keep alert and pray. Otherwise temptation will overpower you. For the spirit indeed is willing, but how weak the body is!...My Father! If this cup cannot go away until I drink it all, your will be done...Sleep on now and take your rest...but no! The time has come! I am betrayed into the hands of evil men! Up! Let's be going! Look! Here comes the man who is betraying me!... My friend, go ahead and do what you have come for...Put away your sword. Those using swords will get killed. Don't you realize that I could ask my Father for thousands of angels to protect us, and he would send them instantly? But if I did, how would the Scriptures be fulfilled that describe what is happening to now?...Am I some dangerous criminal that you had to arm yourselves with swords and clubs before you could arrest me? I was with you teaching daily in the Temple and you didn't stop me then. But this is all happening to fulfill the words of the prophets as recorded in the Scriptures...Yes, I am. And in the future you will see me, the Messiah, sitting at the right hand of God and returning on the clouds of heaven (Jesus accused of blasphemy).

Matthew 27 Judas repents for his betrayal...

Matthew 27:11 Yes (in response to the question if he is the Jews' Messiah).

In these passages we have everything leading up to Jesus' death on the cross that we saw in Mark's Gospel. We have to try to avoid living by swords if we expect not to die by them, and we have to be open to things that do not fit our tiny conceptions of reality. Here, even Jesus was accused of blasphemy, but he held true to his individuation process no matter what came his way. The next time someone brings something to your attention that appears to go against what you believe, instead of immediately killing it, try to consider its merits before judging it.

Judas does repent for his betrayal, and there are many commentaries about that. All I can say is that if he was made to do it by forces beyond him or if he was sincere in his apology, I believe he would be forgiven even for that type of act (even if Dante might argue[53]!). The Cosmic Self/God cares more

---

53.  referring to where betrayers are placed in the circles of hell; see H. Luke – Dark Wood to White Rose

about development and transformation than particular actions, though both need to be proper (see the stories of King David and St. Paul, for example; both were murderers and other negative things but repented and became among the greatest of figures).

Matthew 27:46 Eli, eli, lama sabachthani (My God, my God, why have you forsaken me?)

The famous quote again…

Matthew 28:9-20 Good morning!… Don't be frightened! Go tell my brothers to leave at once for Galilee, to meet me there…I have been given all authority in heaven and earth. Therefore go and make disciples in all the nations, baptizing them into the name of the Father and the Son and of the Holy Spirit, and then teach these new disciples to obey all the commands I have given you; **and be sure of this-that I am with you always, even to the end of the world (age).**

Jesus rises and fulfills his individuation process. He says he will be with us until the end of the age, which is the standard translation. Astrologically, we are shifting from the Age of Pisces to the Age of Aquarius, and this is the backdrop for the shift from the Jesus evolutionary state to that of the Holy Spirit. In other words, we can no longer rely on an external figure or organization, but rather must find the Holy Spirit within if we are to individuate. Because we are in an apocalyptic period (transition moment), there are many confused people trying (or not trying) to find their respective ways today. We must turn to the Self for guidance.

## Luke (Symbol: Ox)

L uke's Gospel is one of the three synoptic ones, and yet it is marked by the famous infancy narrative, which is its hallmark. The incarnation of God is absolutely crucial, psychologically speaking, and that story is told in great detail here. Why it matters so much will have to wait for our analysis of John's Gospel, but there is a key passage from this section that I would like to present here:

Luke 2:9-14 **Suddenly an angel appeared among them, and the landscape shone bright with the glory of the Lord. They were badly frightened, but the angel reassured them. Don't be afraid! he said. I bring you the greatest news ever announced, and it is for everyone! The Savior-yes, the Messiah, the Lord-has been born tonight in Bethlehem! How will you recognize him? You will find a baby wrapped in a blanket, lying in a manger! Suddenly, the angel was joined by a vast host of others-the armies of heaven-praising God. Glory to God in the highest heaven, they sang, and peace on earth for all those pleasing him**[54].

This is the true meaning of Christmas. It is also one of the most well-known passages from all the Gospels. Everyone expected a regal king, but Jesus arrived in the messiest way possible, in a filthy stable. Where difficulty exists, Jesus (the Self) is there, waiting to be followed in the way meant for each individual. Transformation cannot occur when things are comfortable. But

---

54.   This is foreshadowed by Isaiah 9

this is for everyone, by his or her path, and it is not dependent upon the label (or lack thereof) given to the approach. Peace is indeed the reward for being true to the Self.

Luke 2:49 But why did you need to search? Didn't you realize that I would be here at the Temple, in my Father's house?

Jesus is being about the work of the Self, and that is indeed exactly where we should expect to find him.

(The temptation of Jesus)

Luke 4:4 It is written in the Scriptures, 'Other things in life are much more important than bread!'

Very true...

Luke 4:8 We must worship God, and him alone. So it is written in the Scriptures.

The Self is primary, not things associated with the ego.

Luke 4:12 The scriptures also say, 'Do not put the Lord your God to a foolish test.'

See previous analysis…

Luke 4:18-19 the Spirit of the Lord is upon me; he has appointed me to preach the Good News to the poor; he has sent me to heal the brokenhearted and to announce that captives shall be released and the blind shall see, that the downtrodden shall be freed from their oppressors, and that God is ready to give blessings to all who come to him.

The Self will indeed bless those who remain true to it.

Luke 4:21 These Scriptures came true today!

They always do!

Luke 4:23-27 Probably you will quote me that proverb, 'Physician, heal yourself'-meaning, 'Why don't you do miracles here in your home town like those you did in Capernaum?' But I solemnly declare to you that no prophet is accepted in his own home town! For example, remember how Elijah the prophet used a miracle to help the widow of Zarephath-a foreigner from the land of Sidon. There were many Jewish widows needing help in those days of famine, for there had been no rain for three and one-half years, and hunger stalked the land; yet Elijah was not sent to them. Or think of the prophet Elisha, who healed Naaman, a Syrian, rather than the many Jewish lepers needing help.

Again, wisdom is rarely recognized around the home area. This is a big reason why trying to play therapist with family and friends is generally a bad idea, for example.

Luke 4:35 Be silent! (he told the demon) Come out!

This was explained in our previous discussion...

Luke 4:43 I must preach the Good News of the Kingdom of God in other places too, for that is why I was sent.

The messages coming from the Cosmic Self (God) are for everyone!

Luke 5:4 Now go out where it is deeper and let down your nets and you will catch a lot of fish!

There are always more pieces of wisdom where things are deeper!

Luke 5:10 Don't be afraid! From now on you'll be fishing for the souls of men!

The same message for the third time.

**Luke 5:13 Of course I will. Be healed.**

Same meaning as prior healing episodes.

**Luke 5:14 Offer the sacrifice Moses' law requires for lepers who are healed. This will prove to everyone that you are well.**

See previous discussion of this episode.

**Luke 5:20 My friend, your sins are forgiven!**

Jesus does this often; connection with the Self can heal many things.

**Luke 5:22-24 Why is it blasphemy? I, the Messiah, have the authority on earth to forgive sins. But talk is cheap-anybody could say that. So I'll prove it to you by healing this man...pick up your stretcher and go on home, for you are healed!**

Actions speak louder than words, and as per usual, Jesus doesn't care about human definitions of blasphemy.

**Luke 5:27 Come and be one of my disciples!**

The Self always beckons...

**Luke 5:31 It is the sick who need a doctor, not those in good health. My purpose is to invite sinners to turn from their sins, not to spend my time with those who think themselves already good enough.**

Jesus spent much of his time around those who needed him most, and he takes this opportunity to chastise those who think they do not require development and transformation.

**Luke 5:34 Do happy men fast? Do wedding guests go hungry while celebrating with the groom? But the time will come when the bridegroom will be killed, then they won't want to eat.**

Jesus notes the importance of being in the moment.

Luke 5:36-39 No one tears off a piece of a new garment to make a patch for an old one. Not only will the new garment be ruined, but the old garment will look worse with a new patch on it! And no one puts new wine into old wineskins, for the new wine bursts the old skins, ruining the skins and spilling the wine. New wine must be put into new wineskins. But no one after drinking the old wine seems to want the fresh and the new. 'The old ways are best,' they say.

Luke's iteration of this episode; the old ways must pass to make room for the new!

> "Man, if indeed thou knowest what thou doest, thou art
> blessed; but if thou knowest not, thou art accursed, and a
> transgressor of the law." (apocryphal insertion at Luke 6)[55]

This apocryphal verse is absolutely critical, because conscious awareness is of the utmost importance. There is no development or transformation without it.

Luke 6:3-5 Don't you read the Scriptures? Haven't you ever read what King David did when he and his men were hungry? He went into the Temple and took the showbread, the special bread that was placed before the Lord, and ate it-illegal as this was-and shared it with others. I am master even of the Sabbath.

Doing what is right in a given context supersedes any human-made law or rule.

Luke 6:8 Come and stand here where everyone can see.

---

55.  C.G. Jung notes this at the following point: [CW 10, para. 676, p. 357]

Jesus wants this situation to be made public, which is rare, but does occur.

Luke 6:9 I have a question for you. Is it right to do good on the Sabbath day, or to do harm? To save life, or to destroy it?

The answer is quite obvious...

Luke 6:10 Reach out your hand.

Same idea as the other healing episodes.

Luke 6:20-38 What happiness there is for you who are poor, for the Kingdom of God is yours! What happiness there is for you who are now hungry, for you are going to be satisfied! What happiness there is for you who weep, for the time will come when you shall laugh with joy! What happiness it is when others hate you and exclude you and insult you and smear your name because you are mine! When that happens, rejoice! Yes, leap for joy! For you will have a great reward awaiting you in heaven. And you will be in good company-the ancient prophets were treated that way too! But, oh, the sorrows that await the rich. For they have their only happiness down here. They are fat and prosperous now, but a time of awful hunger is before them. Their careless laughter now means sorrow then. And what sadness is ahead for those praised by the crowds-for *false* prophets have *always* been praised. Listen, all of you Love your *enemies*. Do *good* to those who *hate* you. Pray for the happiness of those who *curse* you; implore God's blessing on those who *hurt* you. If someone slaps you on one cheek, let him slap the other too! If someone demands your coat, give him your shirt besides. Give what you have to anyone who asks you for it; and when things are taken away from you, don't worry about getting them back.

Treat others as you want them to treat you. Do you think you deserve credit for merely loving those who love you? Even the godless do that! And if you do good only to those who do you good-is that so wonderful? Even sinners do that much! And if you lend money only to those who can repay you, what good is that? Even the most wicked will lend to their own kind for full return! Love your enemies! Do good to them! Lend to them! And don't be concerned about the fact that they won't repay. Then your reward from heaven will be very great, and you will truly be acting as sons of God: for he is kind to the *unthankful* and to those who are *very wicked*. Try to show as much compassion as your Father does. Never criticize or condemn-or it will all come back on you. Go easy on others; then they will do the same for you. For if you give, you will get! Your gift will return to you in full and overflowing measure, pressed down, shaken together to make room for more, and running over. Whatever measure you use to give-large or small-will be used to measure what is given back to you.

These are all points that have been discussed previously, but there is extra emphasis here on equal and opposite reactions as well as *karma*. God/nature will show you the face you show it.

Luke 6:39-49 What good is it for one blind man to lead another? He will fall into a ditch and pull the other down with him. How can a student know more than his teacher? But if he works hard, he may learn as much. And why quibble about the speck in someone else's eye-his little fault-when a board is in your own? How can you think of saying to him, 'Brother, let me help you get rid of that speck in your eye,' when you can't see past the board in yours? Hypocrite! First get rid of the board, and then perhaps you can see well enough to deal with his speck! A tree from good stock doesn't produce scrub fruit nor do trees from poor stock produce choice fruit. A tree is identified by the kind of fruit it produces. Figs never grow on thorns, or grapes on bramble bushes. A good man produces good deeds from a good heart. And an evil man produces evil deeds from his hidden wickedness. Whatever is in the heart overflows into speech. So why do you call me 'Lord' when you won't obey me? But all those who come and listen and obey me are like a man who builds a house on a strong foundation laid upon the underlying rock. When the floodwaters rise and break against the house, it stands firm, for it is strongly built. But those who listen and don't obey are like a man who builds a house without a foundation. When the floods sweep down against that house, it crumbles into a heap of ruins.

We have also seen all of this before, but Jung has an excellent quote tying things together:

> Therefore, if I am sensible, I shall put myself right first.
> For this I need-because outside authority no longer means anything to me-a knowledge of the innermost foundations of my being, in order that I may base myself firmly on the eternal facts of the human psyche.
> (C.G. Jung)[56]

Luke 7:9 Never among all the Jews in Israel have I met a man with faith like this.

Jesus heals the Roman army captain's slave due to his faith. It is again an "outsider" who gets it right.

---

56.   C.G. Jung – Civilization in Transition [CW 10, para. 462, p. 230]

Luke 7:13-14 Don't cry!...Laddie, come back to life again.

Jesus raises a boy from the dead. An encounter with the Self can also raise us from the "dead," psychologically speaking.

Luke 7:20-23 Go back to John and tell him all you have seen and heard here today: how those who were blind can see. The lame are walking without a limp. The lepers are completely healed. The deaf can hear again. The dead come back to life. And the poor are hearing the Good News. And tell him, 'Blessed is the one who does not lose his faith in me.'

Jesus wants John the Baptist to know what has been happening and to keep the faith himself.

Luke 7:24-28 Who is this man you went out into the Judean wilderness to see? Did you find him weak as grass, moved by every breath of wind? Did you find him dressed in expensive clothes? No! Men who live in luxury are found in palaces, not out in the wilderness. But did you find a prophet? Yes! And more than a prophet. He is the one to whom the Scriptures refer when they say, 'Look! I am sending my messenger ahead of you, to prepare the way before you.' In all humanity there is no one greater than John. And yet the least citizen of the Kingdom of God is greater than he.

Jesus makes explicit who John the Baptist is, and he certainly won't be found in anything resembling a high-end area. But Jesus also reminds us of the importance of humility here; he acknowledges who John is and what he has done, but notes that even he can't be compared to those who have reached the Kingdom via successfully navigating their individuation processes.

Luke 7:31-35 What can I say about such men? With what shall I compare them? They are like a group of children who complain to their friends, 'You don't like it if we play 'wedding' and you don't like it if we play 'funeral!'' For John the Baptist used to go without food and never took a drop of liquor all his life, and you said, 'he must be crazy!' But I eat my food and drink my wine, and you say, 'what a glutton Jesus is! And he drinks! And has the lowest sort of friends!' But I am sure you can always justify your inconsistencies.

Jesus is frustrated that nothing is good enough for some people and that they flip-flop about their complaints. The lack of maturity is evident.

Luke 7:40 Simon (to the Pharisee), I have something to say to you...A man loaned money to two people-$5,000 to one and $500 to the other. But neither of them could pay him back, so he kindly forgave them both, letting them keep the money! Which do you suppose loved him most after that?...Correct (regarding the one who had received the most)...Look! See this woman kneeling here! When I entered your home, you didn't bother to offer me water to wash the dust from my feet, but she has washed them with her tears and wiped them with her hair. You refused me the customary kiss of greeting, but she has kissed my feet again and again from the time I first came in. You neglected the usual courtesy of olive oil to anoint my head, but she has covered my feet with rare perfume. Therefore her sins-and they are many-are forgiven, for she loved me much; but one who is forgiven little, shows little love...your sins are forgiven (to her)... your faith has saved you; go in peace.

Forgiveness and hospitality are very important, and being receptive to the Self is critical. This woman is far from perfect, but she nurtures and cares for Jesus (the Self), and by doing so gains freedom, development, transformation, and peace.

Luke 8:5-15 A farmer went out to his field to sow grain. As he scattered the seed on the ground, some of it fell on a footpath and was trampled on; and the birds came and ate it as it lay exposed. Other seed fell on shallow soil with rock beneath. This seed began to grow, but soon withered and died for lack of moisture. Other seed landed in thistle patches, and the young grain stalks were soon choked out. Still other fell on fertile soil; this seed grew and produced a crop one hundred times as large as he had planted. If anyone has listening ears, use them now! God has granted you to know the meaning of these parables, for they tell a great deal about the Kingdom of God. But these crowds hear the words and do not understand, just as the ancient prophets predicted. This is its meaning: the seed is God's message to men. The hard path where some seed fell represents the hard hearts of those who hear the words of God, but then the devil comes and steals the words away and prevents people from believing and being saved. The stony ground represents those who enjoy listening to sermons, but somehow the message never really gets through to them and doesn't take root and grow. They know the message is true, and sort of believe for awhile; but when the hot winds of persecution blow, they lose interest. The seed among the thorns represents those who listen and believe God's words but whose faith afterwards is choked out by worry and riches and the responsibilities and pleasures of life. And so they are never able to help anyone else to believe the Good News.

But the good soil represents honest, good-hearted people. They listen to God's words and cling to them and steadily spread them to others who also soon believe.

Luke's iteration of the parable of the Sower; note how self-transformation spreads to others here.

Luke 8:16-18 Who ever heard of someone lighting a lamp and then covering it up to keep it from shining? No, lamps are mounted in the open where they can be seen. This illustrates the fact that someday everything [in men's hearts] shall be brought to light and made plain to all. So be careful how you listen; for whoever has, to him shall be given more; and whoever does not have, even what he thinks he has shall be taken away from him.

Gifts, abilities, and resources must shine for all to see and be put to good use. This also refers to the importance of conscious awareness, which must shine for the purpose of development and transformation. Nothing is concealed that will not eventually be revealed, and those lacking awareness or burying their lights/talents will lose even what they have, while those who shine in these ways will become even more blessed, as it were. And how often do we defensively hold on to some attitude or way of being, thinking we have something, only to find it empty and devoid of value?

Luke 8:21 My mother and my brothers are all those who hear the message of God and obey it.

Luke 8:25 Where is your faith? (storm at sea)

These two verses are repeats of earlier episodes we discussed...

Luke 8:30 What is your name? (to a demon)

Naming things of this nature is important; see Mark's Gospel for further discussion.

Luke 8:39 Go back to your family, and tell them what a wonderful thing God has done for you. (to demon-possessed man)

Here, Jesus wants his work to be known, but within a limited sphere.

Luke 8:45 Who touched me?...No, it was someone who deliberately touched me, for I felt healing power go out from me...Daughter, your faith has healed you. Go in peace.

Jesus is touched by a woman with the requisite faith in the Self to be healed.

Luke 8:50 Don't be afraid! Just trust me, and she'll be all right... Stop the weeping! She isn't dead; she is only asleep!...Get up, little girl!

Jesus heals Jairus' daughter; again, it is an outsider who recognizes what can happen via connection to the Self.

Luke 9:3-5 Don't even take along a walking stick, nor a beggar's bag, nor food, nor money. Not even an extra coat. Be a guest in only one home at each village. If the people of a town won't listen to you when you enter it, turn around and leave, demonstrating God's anger against it by shaking its dust from your feet as you go.

This is Luke's version of the excess baggage and shaking dust/ leaving issues that we already noted and are so important.

Luke 9:13-15 You feed them!...just tell them to sit down on the ground in groups of about fifty each.

Third iteration of the loaves and fishes episode...

Luke 9:18-22 Who are the people saying I am?...Who do you think I am?... for I, the Messiah, must suffer much, and be rejected by the Jewish leaders-the elders, chief priests, and teachers of the Law-and be killed; and three days later I will come back to life again!

Jesus cares about who his followers think he is and not just what the masses think. The individual relationship with God is so crucial. Jesus also predicts his passion and resurrection.

Luke 9:23-27 Anyone who wants to follow me must put aside his own desires and conveniences and carry his cross with him every day and *keep close to me*! Whoever loses his life for my sake will save it, but whoever insists on keeping his life will lose it; and what profit is there in gaining the whole world when it means forfeiting one's self? When I, the Messiah, come in my glory and in the glory of the Father and the holy angels, I will be ashamed then of all who are ashamed of me and of my words now. But this is the simple truth-some of you who are standing here right now will not die until you have seen the Kingdom of God.

Luke says the same things we have already observed, and we absolutely have to grasp the importance of carrying our crosses and making the Self primary compared to the ego.

Luke 9:41 O you stubborn faithless people, how long should I put up with you? Bring him here.

Jesus heals a boy possessed by a demon while addressing the disciples.

Luke 9:44 Listen to me and remember what I say. I, the Messiah, am going to be betrayed.

Jesus predicts Judas' actions and his own passion.

Luke 9:47-48 Anyone who takes care of a little child like this is caring for me! And whoever cares for me is caring for God who sent me. Your care for others is the measure of your greatness.

We have to find God everywhere and show care for people, which is usually best accomplished by developing our own awareness and addressing our own issues.

Luke 9:50 You shouldn't have done that! For anyone who is not against you is for you.

The disciples rebuke others casting out demons, but Jesus knows they are all on the same team, as it were, and should act like it.

Luke 9:58 Remember, I don't even own a place to lay my head. Foxes have dens to live in, and birds have nests, but I, the Messiah, have no earthly home at all.

The Self is not constrained by time and space and does not establish a foundation point that is bound in this way.

Luke 9:60 Let those without eternal life concern themselves with things like that. Your duty is to come and preach the coming of the Kingdom of God to all the world.

Again, ego concerns must take a back seat to those of the Self.

Luke 9:62 Anyone who lets himself be distracted from the work I plan for him is not fit for the Kingdom of God.

Pay attention to the Self, not the ego alone with all its distractions.

Luke 10:2-16 Plead with the Lord of the harvest to send out more laborers to help you, for the harvest is so plentiful and the workers so few. Go now, and remember that I am sending you out as lambs among wolves. Don't take any money with you, or a beggar's bag, or even an extra pair of shoes. And don't waste time along the way. Whenever you enter a home, give it your blessing. If it is worthy of the blessing, the blessing will stand; if not, the blessing will return to you. When you enter a village, don't shift around from home to home, but stay in one place, eating and drinking, without question whatever is set before you. And don't hesitate to accept hospitality, for the workman is worthy of his wages! If a town welcomes you, follow these two rules: (1) Eat whatever is set before you. (2) Heal the sick; and as you heal them, say, 'the Kingdom of God is very near you now.' But if a town refuses you, go out into its streets and say, 'we wipe the dust of your town from our feet as a public announcement of your doom. Never forget how close you were to the Kingdom of God! Even wicked Sodom will be better off than such a city on the Judgment Day. What horrors await you, you cities of Chorazin and Bethsaida! For if the miracles I did for you had been done in the cities of Tyre and Sidon, their people would have sat in deep repentance long ago, clothed in sackcloth and throwing ashes on their heads to show their remorse. Yes, Tyre and Sidon will receive less punishment on the Judgment Day than you. And you people of Capernaum, what shall I say about you? Will you be exalted to heaven? No, you shall be brought down to hell. Those who welcome you are welcoming me. And those who reject you are rejecting me. And those who reject me are rejecting God who sent me.

This is a more detailed outline and explanation of the leaving baggage behind and shaking dust/leaving themes. We have already heard these things in our prior examinations of the Gospel material. Development and transformation in context of the Self is an all-hands-on-deck endeavor.

Luke 10:18-20 Yes, I saw Satan falling from heaven as a flash of lightning! And I have given you authority over all the power of the Enemy, and to walk among serpents and scorpions and to crush them. Nothing shall injure you! However, the important thing is not that demons obey you, but that your names are registered as citizens of heaven.

This passage is somewhat of an enigma, but Jesus is pretty clear that sticking by the Self is the way to navigate our experiences. We just need to invest energy in our own individuation processes so we can achieve a state of Heaven; having power over things isn't as important.

Luke 10:21-22 I praise you, O Father, Lord of heaven and earth, for hiding these things from the intellectuals and worldly wise and for revealing them to those who are as trusting as little children. Yes, thank you, Father, for that is the way you wanted it. I am the Agent of my Father in everything; and no one really knows the Son except the Father, and no one really knows the Father except the Son and those to whom the Son chooses to reveal him.

This we have already seen. How often the wise are foolish and the foolish are wise! And of course, no one can fully know God; it is like a limit in calculus or Plato's allegory of the cave.

Luke 10:23-24 How privileged you are to see what you have seen. Many a prophet and king of old has longed for these days, to see and hear what you have seen and heard!

Pretty self-explanatory...

Luke 10:26-36 What does Moses' law say about it?...Right! Do this and you shall live! (man trying to justify his lack of love for certain people)...A Jew going on a trip from Jerusalem to Jericho was attacked by bandits. They stripped him of his clothes and money and beat him up and left him lying half dead beside the road. By chance a Jewish priest came along; and when he saw the man lying there, he crossed to the other side of the road and passed him by. A Jewish Temple-assistant walked over and looked at him lying there, but then went on. But a despised Samaritan came along, and when he saw him, he felt deep pity. Kneeling beside him the Samaritan soothed his wounds with medicine and bandaged them. Then he put the man on his donkey and walked along beside him till they came to an inn, where he nursed him through the night. The next day he handed the innkeeper two twenty-dollar bills and told him to take care of the man. 'I'll pay the difference the next time I am here.' Now which of these three would you say was a neighbor to the bandits' victim?...Yes, now go and do the same.

This is the famous Good Samaritan story, and the lesson is that we must show mercy and compassion to be good neighbors to those around us. And yet again, it is an "outsider" who gets it right.

Luke 10:41 Martha, dear friend, you are so upset over all these details! There is really only one thing worth being concerned about. Mary has discovered it-and I won't take it away from her!

This is the famous Martha and Mary episode. Mary, though she appears lazy, is actually keeping her attention on the Self while Martha, who is doing the bulk of the work, is a bit too focused on concerns of the ego. The point is that while both are important, the Self has to take precedence over the ego in terms of priorities.

Luke 11:2 'Father, may your name be honored for its holiness; send your Kingdom soon. Give us our food day by day. And forgive our sins-for we have forgiven those who sinned against us. And don't allow us to be tempted.'

The most famous Christian prayer again, the Our Father. We'll get to a deeper discussion of this in John's Gospel.

Luke 11:5-14 Suppose you went to a friend's house at midnight, wanting to borrow three loaves of bread. You would shout up to him, 'A friend of mine has just arrived for a visit and I've nothing to give him to eat.' He would call down from his bedroom, 'Please don't ask me to get up. The door is locked for the night and we are all in bed. I just can't help you this time. But I'll tell you this-though he won't do it as a friend, if you keep knocking long enough he will get up and give you everything you want-just because of your persistence. And so it is with prayer- keep on asking and you will keep on getting; keep on looking and you will keep on finding; knock and the door will be opened. Everyone who asks, receives; all who seek, find; and the door is opened to everyone who knocks. You men who are fathers-if your boy asks for bread, do you give him a stone? If he asks for fish, do you give him a snake? If he asks for an egg, do you give him a scorpion? [Of course not!] And if even sinful persons like yourselves give children what they need, don't you realize that your heavenly Father will do at least as much, and give the Holy Spirit to those who ask for him?

Jesus notes the importance of persistence here. Quantum leaps and latent learning work the exact way. The squeaky wheel often does get the grease.

Luke 11:17-26 Any kingdom filled with civil war is doomed; so is a home filled with argument and strife. Therefore, if what you say is true, that Satan is fighting against himself by empowering me to cast out his demons, how can his kingdom survive? And if I am empowered by Satan, what about your own followers? For they cast out demons! Do you think this proves they are possessed by Satan? Ask *them* if you are right! But if I am casting out demons because of power from God, it proves that the Kingdom of God has arrived. For when Satan, strong and fully armed, guards his palace, it is safe-until someone stronger and better-armed attacks and overcomes him and strips him of his weapons and carries off his belongings. Anyone who is not for me is against me; if he isn't helping me, he is hurting my cause. When a demon is cast out of a man, it goes to the deserts, searching there for rest; but finding none, it returns to the person it left, and finds that its former home is all swept and clean. Then it goes and gets seven other demons more evil than itself, and they all enter the man. And so the poor fellow is seven times worse off than he was before.

Here is Luke's version of a house divided not being able to stand (and this is most important within ourselves), the Satan fighting himself issue (which has to be unraveled since, as noted previously, it applies to God as well, and because we have a split here that isn't accurate as directly stated), and the relapse/repression/suppression problem. We already discussed all of these areas to the extent possible prior to reaching John's Gospel.

Luke 11:28 Yes, but even more blessed are all who hear the Word of God and put it into practice.

Insight is hard; action is harder!

Luke 11:29-36 These are evil times, with evil people. They keep asking for some strange happening in the skies [to prove I am the Messiah], but the only proof I will give them is a miracle like that of Jonah, whose experiences proved to the people of Nineveh that God had sent him. My similar experience will prove that God has sent me to these people. And at the Judgment Day the Queen of Sheba shall arise and point her finger at this generation, condemning it, for she went on a long, hard journey to listen to the wisdom of Solomon; but one far greater than Solomon is here [and few pay any attention]. The men of Nineveh, too, shall arise and condemn this nation, for they repented at the preaching of Jonah; and someone far greater than Jonah is here [but this nation won't listen]. No one lights a lamp and hides it! Instead, he puts it on a lampstand to give light to all who enter the room. Your eyes light up your inward being. A pure eye lets sunshine into your soul. A lustful eye shuts out the light and plunges you into darkness. So watch out that the sunshine isn't blotted out. If you are filled with light within, with no dark corners, then your face will be radiant too, as though a floodlight is beamed upon you.

Again, no sign but the sign of Jonah: surrender-dark night of the soul[57]-transformation. The Queen of Sheba is mentioned in the same context as before, and we yet again see the importance of conscious awareness and letting our abilities shine.

Luke 11:39-45 You Pharisees wash the outside, but inside you are still dirty-full of greed and wickedness! Fools! Didn't

---

57.   This was the way St. John of the Cross described his experience.

God make the inside as well as the outside? Purity is best demonstrated by generosity. But woe to you Pharisees! For though you are careful to tithe even the smallest part of your income, you completely forget about justice and the love of God. You should tithe, yes, but you should not leave these other things undone. Woe to you Pharisees! For how you love the seats of honor in the synagogues and the respectful greetings from everyone as you walk through the markets! Yes, awesome judgment is awaiting you. For you are like hidden graves in a field. Men go by you with no knowledge of the corruption they are passing.

Jesus again denounces the hypocrisy and rotten character of the Pharisees as previously noted.

Luke 11:46-52 Yes, the same horrors await you! For you crush men beneath impossible religious demands-demands that you yourselves would never think of trying to keep. Woe to you! For you are exactly like your ancestors who killed the prophets long ago. Murderers! You agree with your fathers that what they did was right-you would have done the same yourselves. This is what God says about you: 'I will send prophets and apostles to you, and you will kill some of them and chase away the others.' And you of this generation will be held responsible for the murder of God's servants from the founding of the world-from the murder of Abel to the murder of Zechariah who perished between the altar and the sanctuary. Yes, it will surely be charged against you. Woe to you experts in religion! For you hide the truth from the people. You won't accept it for yourselves, and you prevent others from having a chance to believe it.

This passage is also a repeat, and Jesus blasts human-made religious rules and dogma as well as hiding the truth from people. So many of us kill the messengers of the Self without even considering the message, and that is an additional error.

Luke 12:1-12 More than anything else, beware of these Pharisees and the way they pretend to be good when they aren't. But such hypocrisy cannot be hidden forever. It will become as evident as yeast in dough. **Whatever they have said in the dark shall be heard in the light, and what you have whispered in the inner rooms shall be broadcast from the housetops for all to hear!** Dear friends, don't be afraid of these who want to murder you. They can only kill the body; they have no power over your souls. But I'll tell you whom to fear-fear God who has the power to kill and then cast into hell. What is the price of five sparrows? A couple of pennies? Not much more than that. Yet God does not forget a single one of them. And he knows the number of hairs on your head! Never fear, you are far more valuable to him than a whole flock of sparrows. And I assure you of this: I, the Messiah, will publicly honor you in the presence of God's angels if you publicly acknowledge me here on earth as your Friend. But I will deny before the angels those who deny me here among men. (Yet those who speak against me may be forgiven-while those who speak against the Holy Spirit shall never be forgiven.) And when you are brought to trial before these Jewish rulers and authorities in the synagogues, don't be concerned about what to say in your defense, for the Holy Spirit will give you the right words even as you are standing there.

All of these points were observed in previous Gospel text, but I would again emphasize that nothing is concealed that will not be revealed. Anything we ignore regarding psychological issues will go into the unconscious, take on a life of its own, and re-emerge in a way that won't be pleasant for us or those around us.

Luke 12:14-59 Man, who made me a judge over you to decide such things as that? Beware! **Don't always be wishing for what you don't have.** For real life and real living are not related to how rich we are. A rich man had a fertile farm that produced fine crops. In fact, his barns were full to overflowing-he couldn't get everything in. He thought about his problem, and finally exclaimed, 'I know-I'll tear down my barns and build bigger ones! Then I'll have room enough. And I'll sit back and say to myself, Friend, you have enough stored away for years to come. Now take it easy! Wine, women, and song for you!' But God said to him, 'Fool! Tonight you die. Then who will get it all?' Yes, every man is a fool who gets rich on earth but not in heaven. Don't worry about whether you have enough food to eat or clothes to wear. For life consists of far more than food and clothes. Look at the ravens-they don't plant or harvest or have barns to store away their food, and yet they get along all right-for God feeds them. And you are far more valuable to him than any birds! And besides, what's the use of worrying? What good does it do? Will it add a single day to your life? Of course not! And if worry can't even do such little things as that, what's the use of worrying over bigger things? Look at the lilies! They don't toil and spin, and yet Solomon in all his glory was not robed as well as they are. And if God provides clothing for the flowers that are here today and gone tomorrow, don't you suppose he will provide clothing for you, you doubters? And don't worry about food-what to eat and drink; don't worry at all that God will provide it for you. All mankind scratches for its daily bread, but your heavenly Father knows your needs. He will always give you all you need from day to day if you will make the Kingdom of God your primary concern. So don't be afraid, little flock. For it gives your Father great happiness to give you the Kingdom. Sell what you have and give to those in need. This will fatten your purses in heaven! And the purses of heaven have no rips or holes in them. Your treasures there will never disappear; no thief can steal them; no moth can destroy them. **Wherever your treasure is, there your heart and thoughts will also be**. Be prepared-all dressed and ready-for your Lord's return from the wedding feast. Then you will be ready to open the door and let him in the moment he arrives and knocks. There will be great joy for those who are ready and waiting for his return. He himself will seat them and put on a waiter's uniform and serve them as they sit and eat! He may come at nine o'clock at night-or even at midnight. But whenever he comes there will be joy for his servants who are ready! Everyone would be ready for him if they knew the exact hour of his return-just as they would be ready for a thief if they knew when he was coming. So be ready all the time. For I, the Messiah, will come when least expected...I'm talking to any faithful, sensible man whose master gives him the responsibility of feeding the other servants. If the master returns and finds that he has done a good job, there will be a reward-his master will put him in charge of all he owns. But if the man begins to think, 'My Lord won't be back for a long time,' and begins to whip the men and women he is supposed to protect, and to spend his time at drinking parties and in drunkenness-well, his master will return without notice and remove him from his position of trust and assign him to the place of the unfaithful. He will be severely punished, for though he knew his duty he refused to do it. But anyone who is not aware that he is doing wrong will be punished only lightly. **Much is required from those to whom much is given, for their responsibility is greater.** I have come to bring fire to the earth, and, oh, that my task were completed! There is a terrible baptism ahead of me, and how I am pent up until it is accomplished! Do you think I have come to give peace to the earth? *No!* Rather, strife and division! From now on families will be split apart, three in favor of me, and two against-or perhaps the other way around. A father will decide one way about me; his son, the other; mother and daughter will disagree; and the decision of an honored mother-in-law will be spurned by her daughter-in-law. When you see clouds beginning to form in the west, you say, 'Here comes a shower.' And you are right. When the south wind blows you say, "Today will be a scorcher." And it is. Hypocrites! You interpret the sky well enough, but you refuse to notice the warnings all around you about the crisis ahead. Why do you refuse to see for yourselves what is right? If you meet your accuser on the way to court, try to settle the matter before it reaches the judge, lest he sentence you to jail; for if that happens you won't be free again until the last penny is paid in full.

There is a lot here, some of which we have already discussed. Jesus notes the critical errors of thinking the grass is greener elsewhere, as it were, and focusing on the ego instead of the Self. He notes that more is expected of those who are given more, be it material or psychospiritual in nature. Jesus again mentions that he is here to bring not peace but a sword, and we analyzed this paradox (compared to other statements) in Matthew's Gospel. He again implores us to be ready and aware as well as to try to settle our disputes.

Luke 13:2-9 Do you think they were worse sinners than other men from Galilee? Is that why they suffered? Not at all! And don't you realize that you also will perish unless you leave your evil ways and turn to God? And what about the eighteen men who died when the Tower of Siloam fell on Jerusalem? Not at all! And you, too, will perish unless you repent. A man planted a fig tree in his garden and came again and again to see if he could find any fruit on it, but he was always disappointed. Finally he told his gardener to cut it down. 'I've waited three years and there hasn't been a single fig!' he said. 'Why bother with it any longer? It's taking up space we can use for something else.' 'Give it one more chance,' the gardener answered. 'Leave it another year, and I'll give it special attention and plenty of fertilizer. If we get figs next year, fine; if not, I'll cut it down.'

The will of the ego has to be sacrificed for the will of the Self, and eventually we must bear fruit via development and transformation.

Luke 13:12-16 Woman, you are healed of your sickness!...You hypocrite! You work on the Sabbath! Don't you untie your cattle from their stalls on the Sabbath and lead them out for water? And is it wrong for me, just because it is the Sabbath day, to free this Jewish woman from the bondage in which Satan has held her for eighteen years?

Jesus isn't going to let a human interpretation of the Sabbath get in the way of healing. But we should all ask ourselves what bondages (complexes) have held us for perhaps many years. I can certainly think of a few in my case...

Luke 13:18-21 What is the Kingdom like? How can I illustrate it? It is like a tiny mustard seed planted in a garden; soon it grows into a tall bush, and the birds live among its branches. It is like yeast kneaded into dough, which works unseen until it has risen high and light.

The mustard seed and yeast parables again...

Luke 13:24-31 The door to heaven is narrow. Work hard to get in, for the truth is that many will try to enter but when the head of the house has locked the door, it will be too late. Then if you stand outside knocking, and pleading, 'Lord, open the door for us,' he will reply, 'I do not know you.' 'But we ate with you, and you taught in our streets,' you will say. And he will reply, 'I tell you, I don't know you. You can't come in here, guilty as you are. Go away.' And there will be great weeping and gnashing of teeth as you stand outside and see Abraham, Isaac, Jacob, and all the prophets within the Kingdom of God-for people will come from all over the world to take their places there. And note this: some who are despised now will be greatly honored then; and some who are highly thought of now will be least important then.

We have already seen these points, and the key is to pay attention to what really matters and to enter through the narrow gate, which indicates just how hard psychological development and transformation is and yet how necessary it is to work towards individuation.

Luke 13:32-35 Go tell that fox (Herod) that I will keep on casting out demons and doing miracles of healing today and tomorrow; and the third day I will reach my destination. Yes, today, tomorrow, and the next day! For it wouldn't do for a prophet of God to be killed except in Jerusalem! O Jerusalem, Jerusalem! The city that murders the prophets. The city that stones those sent to help her. How often I have wanted to gather your children together even as a hen protects her brood under her wings, but you wouldn't let me. And now-now your house is left desolate. And you will never again see me until you say, 'Welcome to him who comes in the name of the Lord.'

Jesus is going to continue his mission until it is finished. He won't let anything, even his passion, get in the way of individuation.

Luke 14:3-5 Well, is it within the law to heal a man on the Sabbath day, or not?...Which of you doesn't work on the Sabbath? If your cow falls into a pit, don't you proceed at once to get it out?

Again, Jesus isn't about human-made laws; he only cares about doing the right thing given the context.

Luke 14:8-14 If you are invited to a wedding feast, don't always head for the best seat. For if someone more respected than you shows up, the host will bring him over to where you are sitting and say, 'Let this man sit here instead.' And you, embarrassed, will have to take whatever seat is left at the foot of the table! Do this instead-start at the foot; and when your host sees you he will come and say, 'Friend, we have a better place than this for you!' Thus you will be honored in front of all the other guests. For everyone who tries to honor himself shall be humbled; and he who humbles himself shall be honored. When you put on a dinner, don't invite friends, brothers, relatives, and rich neighbors! For they will return the invitation. Instead, invite the poor, the crippled, the lame, and the blind. Then at the resurrection of the godly, God will reward you for inviting those who can't repay you.

Humbleness is a prerequisite for following the Self, as is not expecting things that gratify the ego in return for good works. This famous passage explicitly illustrates these points.

Luke 14:16-24 A man prepared a great feast and sent out many invitations. When all was ready, he sent his servant around to notify the guests that it was time for them to arrive. But they all began making excuses. One said he had just bought a field and wanted to inspect it, and asked to be excused. Another said he had just bought five pair of oxen and wanted to try them out. Another had just been married and for that reason couldn't come. The servant returned and reported to his master what they had said. His master was angry and told him to go quickly into the streets and alleys of the city and to invite the beggars, crippled, lame, and blind. But even then, there was still room. 'Well, then,' said his master, 'go out into the country lanes and out behind the hedges and urge anyone you find to come, so that the house will be full. For none of those I invited first will get even the smallest taste of what I had prepared for them.'

We saw this episode before. How often do we make excuses on account of the ego instead of the Self?

Luke 14:26-35 Anyone who wants to be my follower must love me far more than he does his own father, mother, wife, children, brothers, or sisters-yes, more than his own life-otherwise he cannot be my disciple. And no one can be my disciple who does not carry his own cross and follow me. But don't begin until you count the cost. For who would begin construction of a building without first getting estimates and then checking to see if he has enough money to pay the bills? Otherwise he might complete only the foundation before running out of funds. And then how everyone would laugh! 'See that fellow there?' they would mock. 'He started that building and ran out of money before it was finished!' Or what king would ever dream of going to war without first sitting down with his counselors and discussing whether his army of 10,000 is strong enough to defeat the 20,000 men who are marching against him? If the decision is negative, then while the enemy troops are still far away, he will send a truce team to discuss terms of peace. So no one can become my disciple unless he first sits down and counts his blessings-and then renounces them all for me. What good is salt that has lost its saltiness? Flavorless salt is fit for nothing-not even for fertilizer. It is worthless and must be thrown out. Listen well, if you would understand my meaning.

Jesus makes clear that the ego has to take a back seat to the Self, and our crosses (shadows and complexes) must be carried. We cannot become flavorless, as noted, or inflated (the salt of the earth is representative of humility as well). However, this journey of development and transformation, though necessary, requires preparation through self-reflection, hard work, and conscious awareness; we have to take a psychological inventory of ourselves before embarking on this most important of quests.

Luke 15:3-32 If you had a hundred sheep and one of them strayed away and was lost in the wilderness, wouldn't you leave the ninety-nine others to go and search for the lost one until you found it? And then you would joyfully carry it home on your shoulders. When you arrived you would call together your friends and neighbors to rejoice with you because your lost sheep was found. Well, in the same way heaven will be happier over one lost sinner who returns to God than over ninety-nine others who haven't strayed away! Or take another illustration: A woman has ten valuable silver coins and loses one. Won't she light a lamp and look in every corner of the house and sweep every nook and cranny until she finds it? And then won't she call in her friends and neighbors to rejoice with her? In the same way there is joy in the presence of the angels of God when one sinner repents…A man had two sons. When the younger told his father, 'I want my share of your estate now, instead of waiting until you die!' his father agreed to divide his wealth between his sons. A few days later this younger son packed all his belongings and took a trip to a distant land, and there wasted all his money on parties and prostitutes. About the time the money was gone a great famine swept over the land, and he began to starve. He persuaded a local farmer to hire him to feed his pigs. The boy became so hungry that even the pods he was feeding the swine looked good to him. And no one gave him anything. When he finally came to his senses, he said to himself, 'At home even the hired men have food enough and to spare, and here I am, dying of hunger!' I will go home to my father and say, 'Father, I have sinned against both heaven and you, and am no longer worthy of being called your son. Please take me on as a hired man.' So he returned home to his father. And while he was still a long distance away, his father saw him coming, and was filled with loving pity and ran and embraced him and kissed him. His son said to him, 'Father, I have sinned against heaven and you, and am not worthy of being called your son.' But his father said to the slaves, 'Quick! Bring the finest robe in the house and put it on him. And a jeweled ring for his finger; and shoes! And kill the calf we have in the fattening pen. We must celebrate with a feast, for this son of mine was dead and has returned to life. He was lost and is found.' So the party began. Meanwhile, the older son was in the fields working; when he returned home, he heard dance music coming from the house, and he asked one of the servants what was going on. 'Your brother is back,' he was told, 'and your father has killed the calf we were fattening and has prepared a great feast to celebrate his coming home again unharmed.' The older brother was angry and wouldn't go in. His father came out and begged him, but he replied, 'All these years I've worked hard for you and never once refused to do a single thing you told me to; and in all that time you never gave me even one young goat for a feast with my friends. Yet when this son of yours comes back after spending your money on prostitutes, you celebrate by killing the finest calf we have on the place.' 'Look, dear son,' his father said to him, 'you and I are very close, and everything I have is yours. But it is right to celebrate. For he is your brother; and he was dead and has come back to life! He was lost and is found!'

The lost sheep, the finding of the coins, and the famous story of the Prodigal Son illustrate the development and transformation that is sought by the Self. Do we have eyes to see, ears to hear, and the courage to act as required?

Luke 16:1-14 A rich man hired an accountant to handle his affairs, but soon a rumor went around that the accountant was thoroughly dishonest. So his employer called him in and said, 'What's this I hear about your stealing from me? Get your report in order, for you are to be dismissed.' The accountant thought to himself, 'Now what? I'm through here, and I haven't the strength to go out and dig ditches, and I'm too proud to beg. I know just the thing! And then I'll have plenty of friends to take care of me when I leave!' So he invited each one who owed money to his employer to come and discuss the situation. He asked the first one, 'How much do you owe him?' 'My debt is 850 gallons of olive oil,' the man replied. 'Yes, here is the contract you signed,' the accountant told him. 'Tear it up and write another one for half that much!' 'And how much do you owe him?' he asked the next man. 'A thousand bushels of wheat,' was the reply. 'Here,' the accountant said, 'take your note and replace it with one for only 800 bushels!' The rich man had to admire the rascal for being so shrewd. And it is true that the citizens of this world are more clever [in dishonesty!] than the godly are. But shall I tell you to act that way, to buy friendship through cheating? Will this ensure your entry into an everlasting home in heaven? No! For unless you are honest in small matters, you won't be in large ones. If you cheat even a little, you won't be honest with greater responsibilities. And if you are untrustworthy about worldly wealth, who will trust you with the true riches of heaven? And if you are not faithful with other people's money, why should you be entrusted with money of your own? **For neither you nor anyone else can serve two masters. You will hate one and show loyalty to the other, or else the other way around-you will be**

**enthusiastic about one and despise the other.** You cannot serve both God and money.

There are two major points here. One is the importance of honesty above almost anything else; you have nothing real without it, and dishonesty is not tolerated by the Self. The other is the idea we saw earlier about the inability to serve two masters. I would phrase it more in terms of prioritizing the Self over the ego (since both matter and everything has its place), but the point is effectively the same. And it certainly is no accident that Jesus uses money as the example of the wrong master.

Luke 16:15-18 (to the Pharisees) You wear a noble, pious expression in public, but God knows your evil hearts. Your pretense brings you honor from the people, but it is an abomination in the sight of God. Until John the Baptist began to preach, the laws of Moses and the messages of the prophets were your guides. But John introduced the Good News that the Kingdom of God would come soon. And now eager multitudes are pressing in. But that doesn't mean that the Law has lost its force in even the smallest point. It is as strong and unshakable as heaven and earth. So anyone who divorces his wife and marries someone else commits adultery, and anyone who marries a divorced woman commits adultery.

These points are repeats of what we saw earlier, but again Jesus clearly shows his disdain for hypocrisy.

Luke 16:19-31 There was a certain rich man, who was splendidly clothed and lived each day in mirth and luxury. One day Lazarus, a diseased beggar, was laid at his door. As he lay there longing for scraps from the rich man's table, the dogs would come and lick his open sores. Finally the beggar died and was carried by the angels to be with Abraham in the place of the righteous dead. The rich man also died and was buried, and his soul went into hell. There, in torment, he saw Lazarus in the far distance with Abraham. 'Father Abraham,' he shouted, 'have some pity! Send Lazarus over here if only to dip the tip of his finger in water and cool my tongue, for I am in anguish in these flames.' But Abraham said to him, 'Son, remember that during your lifetime you had everything you wanted, and Lazarus had nothing. So now he is here being comforted and you are in anguish. And besides, there is a great chasm separating us, and anyone wanting to come to you from here is stopped at its edge; and no one over there can cross to us.' Then the rich man said, 'O Father Abraham, then please send him to my father's home-for I have five brothers-to warn them about this place of torment lest they come here when they die.' But Abraham said, 'the Scriptures have warned them again and again. Your brothers can read them any time they want to.' The rich man replied, 'no, Father Abraham, they won't bother to read them. But if someone is sent to them from the dead, then they will turn from their sins.' But Abraham said, 'If they won't listen to Moses and the prophets, they won't listen even though someone rises from the dead.'

The first shall be last and the last shall be first. Jesus knows the truth of the concept of enantiodromia (conversion into the opposite). Here, it appears that the rich man's actions, even though he now feels remorse, are part of a family pattern, and no one seems able to break the cycle. This happens multigenerationally in all family systems, and it can take the activation of the hero function or other major intervention in one or more members to reverse the destructive pattern(s). I'm not so sure, however, that people would ignore someone rising from the dead, especially if it was Jesus, appearing to them with a message. At least some would likely pay attention...

Luke 17:1-4 There will always be temptations to sin, but woe to the man who does the tempting. If he were thrown into the sea with a huge rock tied to his neck, he would be far better off than facing the punishment in store for those who harm these little children's souls. I am warning you! Rebuke your brother if he sins, and forgive him if he is sorry. Even if he wrongs you seven times a day and each time turns again and asks forgiveness, forgive him.

These points were already noted in prior Gospel material...

Luke 17:6-10 If your faith were only the size of a mustard seed, it would be large enough to uproot that mulberry tree over there and send it hurtling into the sea! Your command would bring immediate results! When a servant comes in from plowing or taking care of sheep, he doesn't just sit down and eat, but first prepares his master's meal and serves him his supper before he eats his own. And he is not even thanked, for he is merely doing what he is supposed to do. Just so, if you merely obey me, you should not consider yourselves worthy of praise. For you have simply done your duty!

Faith can move mountains as they say, but that isn't a literal truth of course. And, praise should not be given for doing what you are *supposed* to do!

Luke 17:14 Go to the Jewish priest and show him that you are healed!

See previous episodes in Mark and Matthew...

Luke 17:17-19 Didn't I heal ten men? Where are the nine? Does only this foreigner return to give glory to God?...Stand up and go; your faith has made you well.

Again, the "outsiders" turn out to be the ones with faith and awareness.

Luke 17:20-37 The Kingdom of God isn't ushered in with visible signs. You won't be able to say, 'It has begun here in this place or there in that part of the country.' **For the Kingdom of God is within you**...the time is coming when you will long for me to be with you even for a single day, but I won't be here. Reports will reach you that I have returned and that I am in this place or that; don't believe it or go out to look for me. For when I return, you will know it beyond all doubt. It will be as evident as the lightning that flashes across the skies. But first I must suffer terribly and be rejected by this whole nation. [When I return] the world will be [as indifferent to the things of God] as the people were in Noah's day. They ate and drank and married-everything just as usual right up to the day when Noah went into the ark and the flood came and destroyed them all. And the world will be as it was in the days of Lot: people went about their daily business-eating and drinking, buying and selling, farming and building-until the morning Lot left Sodom. Then fire and brimstone rained down from heaven and destroyed them all. Yes, it will be 'business as usual' right up to the hour of my return. Those away from home that day must not return to pack; those in the fields must not return to town-remember what happened to Lot's wife! Whoever clings to his life shall lose it, and whoever loses his life shall save it. That night two men will be asleep in the same room, and one will be taken away, the other left. Two women will be working together at household tasks; one will be taken, the other left; and so it will be with men working side by side in the fields...where the body is, the vultures gather!

This passage contains apocalyptic/eschatological material with more detail about the state of things upon the return of Jesus. We have observed some of this previously, but there is the very critical point here that *the Kingdom is within*. This is precisely true from a psychological standpoint.

Luke 18:2-8 There was a city judge, a very godless man who had great contempt for everyone. A widow of that city came to him frequently to appeal for justice against a man who had harmed her. The judge ignored her for a while, but eventually she got on his nerves. 'I fear neither God nor man,' he said to himself, 'but this woman bothers me. I'm going to see that she gets justice, for she is wearing me out with her constant coming! If even an evil judge can be worn down like that, don't you think that God will surely give justice to his people who plead with him day and night?' Yes! He will answer them quickly! But the question is: when I, the Messiah, return, how many will I find who have faith [and are praying]?

For those who are persistent and faithful to the Self, great persuasion is possible!

Luke 18:10-14 Two men went to the Temple to pray. One was a proud, self-righteous Pharisee, and the other a cheating tax collector. The proud Pharisee 'prayed' this prayer: 'Thank God, I am not a sinner like everyone else, especially like that tax collector over there! For I never cheat, I don't commit adultery, I go without food twice a week, and I give to God a tenth of everything I earn.' But the corrupt tax collector stood at a distance and dared not even lift his eyes to heaven as he prayed, but beat upon his chest in sorrow, exclaiming, 'God, be merciful to me, a sinner.' I tell you, this sinner, not the Pharisee, returned home forgiven! For the proud shall be humbled, but the humble shall be honored.

We should all pray for mercy, not just because humility is a virtue, but because we all need it to a certain extent.

Luke 18:16-17 Let the little children come to me! Never send them away! For the Kingdom of God belongs to men who have hearts as trusting as these little children's. And anyone who doesn't have their kind of faith will never get within the Kingdom's gates.

See Mark's Gospel for the childlike attitude discussion.

Luke 18:19-30 Do you realize what you are saying when you call me 'good?' Only God is truly good, and no one else. But as to your question, you know what the ten commandments say-don't commit adultery, don't murder, don't steal, don't lie, honor your parents, and so on...there is still one thing you lack. Sell all you have and give the money to the poor-it will become treasure for you in heaven-and come, follow me...How hard it is for the rich to enter the Kingdom of God! It is easier for a camel to go through the eye of a needle than for a rich man to enter the Kingdom of God....God can do what men can't!...Yes, and everyone who has done as you have, leaving home, wife, brothers, parents, or children for the sake of the Kingdom of God, will be repaid many times over now, as well as receiving eternal life in the world to come.

Again, see Mark's Gospel for analysis...

Luke 18:31-33 As you know, we are going to Jerusalem. And when we get there, all the predictions of the ancient prophets concerning me will come true. I will be handed over to the Gentiles to be mocked and treated shamefully and spat upon, and lashed and killed. And the third day I will rise again.

Jesus predicts his passion and resurrection.

Luke 18:40-42 Bring the blind man over here....What do you want?...All right, begin seeing. Your faith has healed you.

Similar meaning as previous episodes...

Luke 19:5-10 Zacchaeus! Quick! Come down! For I am going to be a guest in your home today!...This shows that salvation has come to this home today. This man was one of the lost sons of Abraham, and I, the Messiah, have come to search for and to save such souls as his.

Because Zacchaeus sought the Self, climbing a tree so he could see Jesus, he was able to transform. We all fail to measure up (pun intended) to some extent, so we also need to be in search of the Self.

Luke 19:12-27 A nobleman living in a certain province was called away to the distant capital of the empire to be crowned king of his province. Before he left he called together ten assistants and gave them each $2,000 to invest while he was gone. But some of his people hated him and sent him their declaration of independence, stating that they had rebelled and would not acknowledge him as their king. Upon his return he called in the men to whom he had given the money, to find out what they had done with it, and what their profits were. The first man reported a tremendous gain-ten times as much as the original amount! 'Fine!' the king exclaimed. 'You are a good man. You have been faithful with the little I entrusted to you, and as your reward, you shall be governor of ten cities.' The next man also reported a splendid gain-five times the original amount. 'All right!' his master said. 'You can be governor over five cities.' But the third man brought back only the money he had started with. 'I've kept it safe,' he said, 'because I was afraid [you would demand my profits], for you are a hard man to deal with, taking what isn't yours and even confiscating the crops that others plant.' 'You vile and wicked slave,' the king roared. 'Hard, am I? That's exactly how I'll be toward you! If you knew so much about me and how tough I am, then why didn't you deposit the money in the bank so that I could at least get some interest on it.' Then turning to the others standing by he ordered, 'Take the money away from him and give it to the man who earned the most.' 'But, sir,' they said, 'he has enough already!' 'Yes,' the king replied, 'but it is always true that those who have little, soon lose even that. And now about these enemies of mine who revolted-bring them in and execute them before me.'

Again, the parable of the talents, with the additional point that rebelling against the Self tends to bring on suffering, and not the transformational kind…

Luke 19:30-31 Untie him (the colt), and bring him here. And if anyone asks you what you are doing, just say, 'The Lord needs him.'

Jesus will ride humbly into Jerusalem on Palm Sunday as previously noted.

Luke 19:40-46 If they keep quiet, the stones along the road will burst into cheers!...Eternal peace was within your reach and you turned it down, and now it is too late (weeping). Your enemies will pile up earth against your walls and encircle you and close in on you, and crush you to the ground, and your children with you; your enemies will not leave one stone upon another-for you have rejected the opportunity God offered you...The Scriptures declare, 'My Temple is a place of prayer; but you have turned it into a den of thieves.'

Jesus laments the lack of eyes to see and ears to hear, and then we again see the episode where he overturns the tables in the Temple.

Luke 20:3-8 I'll ask you a question before I answer. Was John sent by God, or was he merely acting under his own authority?... then I won't answer your question either.

Again, no games.

Luke 20:9-18 A man planted a vineyard and rented it out to some farmers, and went away to a distant land to live for several years. When harvest time came, he sent one of his men to the farm to collect his share of the crops. But the tenants beat him up and sent him back empty-handed. Then he sent another, but the same thing happened; he was beaten up and insulted and sent away without collecting. A third man was sent and the same thing happened. He, too, was wounded and chased away. 'What shall I do?' the owner asked himself. 'I know! I'll send my cherished son. Surely they will show respect for him.' But when the tenants saw his son, they said, 'This is our chance! This fellow will inherit all the land when his father dies. Come on. Let's kill him, and then it will be ours.' So they dragged him out of the vineyard and killed him. What do you think the owner will do? I'll tell you-he will come and kill them and rent the vineyard to others...Then what does the Scripture mean where it says, '**The Stone rejected by the builders was made the cornerstone?**' Whoever stumbles over that Stone shall be broken; and those on whom it falls will be crushed to dust.

This story was discussed in prior Gospel material. And again we have the point that the despised stone (e.g. Jesus, the Philosopher's Stone, the Self, etc.) is actually the valued foundation.

Luke 20:24-25 Show me a coin. Whose portrait is this on it? And whose name?...Then give the emperor all that is his-and give to God all that is his!

Again, give Caesar what is Caesar's and God what is God's, as previously noted.

Luke 20:34-47 Marriage is for people here on earth, but when those who are counted worthy of being raised from the dead get to heaven, they do not marry. And they never die again; in these respects they are like angels, and are sons of God, for they are raised up in new life from the dead. But as to your real question-whether or not there is a resurrection-why, even the writings of Moses himself prove this. For when he describes how God appeared to him in the burning bush, he speaks of God as 'the God of Abraham, the God of Isaac, and the God of Jacob.' To say that the Lord *is* some person's God means that person is *alive*, not dead! So from God's point of view, all men are living... Why is it that Christ, the Messiah, is said to be a descendant of King David? For David himself wrote in the book of Psalms: 'God said to my Lord, the Messiah, "Sit at my right hand until I place your enemies beneath your feet."' How can the Messiah be both David's son and David's God at the same time?...Beware of these experts in religion, for they love to parade in dignified robes and to be bowed to by the people as they walk along the street. And how they love the seats of honor in the synagogues and at religious festivals! But even while they are praying long prayers with great outward piety, they are planning schemes to cheat widows out of their property. Therefore God's heaviest sentence awaits these men.

All of these points were discussed in prior areas of the Gospel text. It might be a good idea to return to those sections if a refresher is needed. But the key is that everything points to the Cosmic Self, which is not bound by time or space; it is the great I AM as indicated.

Luke 21:3-4 Really this poor widow has given more than all the rest of them combined. For they have given a little of what they didn't need, but she, poor as she is, has given everything she has.

Again, 100% effort is required for development and transformation.

Luke 21:6-36 The time is coming when all these things you are admiring will be knocked down, and not one stone will be left on top of another; all will become one vast heap of rubble...Don't let anyone mislead you. For many will come announcing themselves as the Messiah, and saying, 'The time has come.' But don't believe them! And when you hear of wars and insurrections beginning, don't panic. True, wars must come, but the end won't follow immediately-for nation shall rise against nation and kingdom against kingdom, and there will be great earthquakes, and famines in many lands, and epidemics, and terrifying things happening in the heavens. But before all this occurs, there will be a time of special persecution, and you will be dragged into synagogues and prisons and before kings and governors for my Name's sake. But as a result, the Messiah will be widely known and honored. Therefore, don't be concerned about how to answer the charges against you, for I will give you the right words and such logic that none of your opponents will be able to reply! Even those closest to you-your parents, brothers, relatives, and friends will betray you and have you arrested; and some of you will be killed. And everyone will hate you because you are mine and are called by my name. But not a hair of your head will perish! **For if you stand firm, you will win your souls.** But when you see Jerusalem surrounded by armies, then you will know that the time of its destruction has arrived. Then let the people of Judea flee to the hills. Let those in Jerusalem try to escape, and those outside the city must not attempt to return. For those will be days of God's judgment, and the words of the ancient scriptures written by the prophets will be abundantly fulfilled. Woe to expectant mothers in those days, and those with tiny babies. For there will be great distress upon this nation and wrath upon this people. They will be brutally killed by enemy weapons, or sent away as exiles and captives to all the nations of the world; and Jerusalem shall be conquered and trampled down by the Gentiles until the period of Gentile triumph ends in God's good time. Then there will be strange events in the skies-warnings, evil omens and portents in the sun, moon, and stars; and down here on earth the nations will be in turmoil, perplexed by the roaring seas and strange tides. The courage of many people will falter because of the fearful fate they see coming upon the earth, for the stability of the very heavens will be broken up. Then the peoples of the earth shall see me, the Messiah, coming in a cloud with power and great glory. So when all these things begin to happen, stand straight and look up! For your salvation is near...Notice the fig tree, or any other tree. When the leaves come out, you know without being told that summer is near. In the same way, when you see the events taking place that I've described you can be just as sure that the Kingdom of God is near. I solemnly declare to you that when these things happen, the end of this age has come. And though all heaven and earth shall pass away, yet my words remain forever true. Watch out! Don't let my sudden coming catch you unawares; don't let me find you living in careless ease, carousing and drinking, and occupied with the problems of this life, like all the rest of the world. Keep a constant watch. And pray that if possible you may arrive in my presence without having to experience these horrors.

This is the apocalyptic/eschatological section of Luke's Gospel, but with emphasis on a very important point about development and transformation: whoever endures until the end will be saved.

Luke 22:10-12 As soon as you enter Jerusalem, you will see a man walking along carrying a pitcher of water. Follow him into the house he enters, and say to the man who lives there, 'Our

Teacher says for you to show us the guest room where he can eat the Passover meal with his disciples.' He will take you upstairs to a large room all ready for us. That is the place. Go ahead and prepare the meal there.

Again, preparing the Last Supper...

Luke 22:15-22 I have looked forward to this hour with deep longing, anxious to eat this Passover meal with you before my suffering begins. For I tell you now that I won't eat it again until what it represents has occurred in the Kingdom of God...Take this and share it among yourselves. For I will not drink wine again until the Kingdom of God has come...This is my body, given for you. Eat it in remembrance of me...This wine is the token of God's new agreement to save you-an agreement sealed with the blood I shall pour out to purchase back your souls. But here at this table, sitting among us as a friend, is the man who will betray me. I must die. It is part of God's plan. But, oh, the horror awaiting that man who betrays me.

Luke's version of the Last Supper...

Luke 22:25-71 In this world the kings and great men order their slaves around, and the slaves have no choice but to like it! But among you, the one who serves you best will be your leader. Out in the world the master sits at the table and is served by his servants. But not here! For I am your servant. Nevertheless, because you have stood true to me in these terrible days, and because my Father has granted me a Kingdom, I, here and now, grant you the right to eat and drink at my table in that Kingdom; and you will sit on thrones judging the twelve tribes of Israel. Simon, Simon, Satan has asked to have you, to sift you like wheat, but I have pleaded in prayer for you that your faith should not completely fail. So when you have repented and turned to me again, strengthen and build up the faith of your brothers...Peter, let me tell you something. Between now and tomorrow morning when the rooster crows, you will deny me three times, declaring that you don't even know me...When I sent you out to preach the Good News and you were without money, duffle bag, or extra clothing, how did you get along?... But now, take a duffle bag if you have one, and your money. And if you don't have a sword, better sell your clothes and buy one! For the time has come for this prophecy about me to come true: 'He will be condemned as a criminal!' Yes, everything written about me by the prophets will come true...Enough!...Pray God that you will not be overcome by temptation...'Father, if you are willing, please take away this cup of horror from me. But I want your will, not mine...Asleep! Get up! Pray God that you will not fall when you are tempted...Judas, how can you do this-betray the Messiah with a kiss?...Don't resist any more (Peter cut off the ear of the High Priest's servant)...Am I a robber, that you have come armed with swords and clubs to get me? Why didn't you arrest me in the Temple? I was there every day. But this is your moment-the time when Satan's power reigns supreme...If I tell you, you won't believe me or let me present my case. But the time is soon coming when I, the Messiah, shall be enthroned beside Almighty God...Yes, I am (the Son of God).

Jesus' time is fast approaching, and we have seen this material before. It is very clear here that we must never, as *Star Wars* points out, underestimate the power of the dark side.

Luke 23:28-46 Daughters of Jerusalem, don't weep for me, but for yourselves and for your children. For the days are coming when the women who have no children will be counted fortunate indeed. Mankind will beg the mountains to fall on them and crush them, and the hills to bury them. For if such things as this are done to me, the Living Tree, what will they do to you?... **Father, forgive these people, for they don't know what they are doing**...(to one criminal beside him on a cross) Today you will be with me in Paradise. This is a solemn promise...**Father, I commit my spirit to you.**

Jesus is crucified between the opposites, the good and the bad thieves. Nothing less can result in development, transformation, and individuation.

Luke 24:17-26 You seem to be in a deep discussion about something. What are you so concerned about?...What things?... you are such foolish, foolish people! You find it so hard to believe all that the prophets wrote in the Scriptures! Wasn't it clearly predicted by the prophets that the Messiah would have to suffer all these things before entering his time of glory?

Jesus cannot forsake his individuation process…

Luke 24:38-49 Why are you frightened? Why do you doubt that it is really I? Look at my hands! Look at my feet! You can see that it is I, myself! Touch me and make sure that I am not a ghost! For ghosts don't have bodies, as you see that I do!...do you have anything here to eat?...When I was with you before, don't you remember my telling you that everything written about me by Moses and the prophets and in the Psalms must all come true?... Yes, it was written long ago that the Messiah must suffer and die and rise again from the dead on the third day; and that this message of salvation should be taken from Jerusalem to all the nations: *There is forgiveness of sins for all who turn to me.* You have seen these prophecies come true. And now I will send the Holy Spirit upon you, just as my Father promised. Don't begin telling others yet-stay here in the city until the Holy Spirit comes and fills you with power from heaven.

Luke's account of some already noted post-resurrection themes...

## John (Symbol: Eagle)

The Gospel according to John is very different from the other three Synoptic Gospels. And it is here that more psychological value is to be found than in any other Gospel. John is well known for the famous lines at John 1:1, 1:14, and 3:16, as well as the Bread of Life discourse. But John 8:32 and John 14:12 are absolutely critical from a psychological standpoint. We begin with three of the most famous biblical passages that exist:

John 1:1 (typical wording) In the beginning was the Word, and the Word was with God, and the Word was God.

The famous beginning of John's Gospel. Jesus is the living Word.

John 1:2-5 He has always been alive and is himself God. **He created everything there is-nothing exists that he didn't make.** Eternal life is in him, and this life gives light to all mankind. His life is the light that shines through the darkness-and the darkness can never extinguish it.

The first five verses of John show a few very important points about the nature of God and reality. First, Dourley[58] is incorrect, based on these lines (which are of such import that they have to be consistent with other statements), in saying that God is created out of the psyche and does not exist *a priori*. By doing this, he contradicts Edinger's Cosmic Self idea discussed earlier

---

58.   see J. Dourley - On Behalf of the Mystical Fool: Jung on the Religious Situation; L. Corbett has a more viable viewpoint in not committing one way or the other due to empirical limitations (see L. Corbett – The God-image in Jung and the Monotheisms: A Study in Contrast – lecture delivered via the C.G. Jung Club of Orange County).

and the firmly established Jungian notion that the ego (conscious human perspective) is subservient to the Self. And at any rate, something had to create the psyche, which is not equivalent to God in the way he is discussing it. Second, this passage indicates that *everything* was created by God. That includes good and evil, and I highly doubt anyone with sound faculties will deny the existence of both good and evil. Third, God (i.e. the Self), is indeed eternal and not bound by time and space, as is the case with archetypes as noted. The life of Jesus, in the Christian tradition, being the highest symbol of the Self in this context, always shines brightly and can never be extinguished, though it can be ignored or denied, leading to many types of significant problems. Hold these thoughts...

John 1:14 And Christ became a human being and lived here on earth among us and was full of loving forgiveness and truth. And some of us have seen his glory-the glory of the only Son of the heavenly Father!

> God's Incarnation in Christ requires continuation and completion because Christ, owing to his virgin birth and his sinlessness, was not an empirical human being at all.... he remained outside and above mankind. Job, on the other hand, was an ordinary human being, and therefore the wrong done to him, and through him to mankind, can, according to divine justice, only be repaired by an incarnation of God in an empirical human being...otherwise there can be no reconciliation between the two.
> (C.G. Jung)[59]

---

59.   C.G. Jung – Answer to Job [CW 11, para. 657, p. 414]

This quote adds the appropriate context to the passage and sets the stage for what is to come.

John 1:38 What do you want? (to people following him)...come and see...You are Simon, John's son-but you shall be called Peter, the rock!...Come with me...Here comes an honest man-a true son of Israel...I could see you under the fig tree before Philip found you...Do you believe all this just because I told you I had seen you under the fig tree? You will see greater proofs than this. You will even see heaven open and the angels of God coming back and forth to me, the Messiah.

These are areas we have already encountered in our examination of the synoptic Gospels.

John 2:4-8 I can't help you now. It isn't yet my time for miracles (wedding feast at Cana)...Dip some out and take it to the master of ceremonies.

Jesus is persuadable by those who believe, and here he performs the very well-known miracle of changing water into wine. The ordinary becomes extraordinary when the Self is involved.

John 2:16 Get these things out of here. Don't turn my Father's house into a market!

Here is that Temple episode again…

John 2:19 All right, this is the miracle I will do for you: Destroy this sanctuary and in three days I will raise it up!

Jesus is speaking of his death and resurrection, not the actual Temple, though of course they do not understand...

John 3:3 With all the earnestness I possess I tell you this: Unless you are born again, you can never get into the Kingdom of God.

We must go through continual cycles of death and rebirth on a new level to advance the individuation process.

John 3:5-21 What I am telling you so earnestly is this: Unless one is born of water and the Spirit, he cannot enter the Kingdom of God. Men can only reproduce human life, but the Holy Spirit gives new life from heaven; so don't be surprised at my statement that you must be born again! Just as you can hear the wind but can't tell where it comes from or where it will go next, so it is with the Spirit. We do not know on whom he will next bestow this life from heaven...(to Nicodemus) You, a respected Jewish teacher, and yet you don't understand these things? I am telling you what I know and have seen-and yet you won't believe me. But if you don't even believe me when I tell you about such things as these that happen here among men, how can you possibly believe if I tell you what is going on in heaven? For only I, the Messiah, have come to earth and will return to heaven again. And as Moses in the wilderness lifted up the bronze image of a serpent on a pole, even so I must be lifted up upon a pole, so that anyone who believes in me will have eternal life. **For God loved the world so much that he gave his only Son so that anyone who believes in him shall not perish but have eternal life**. God did not send his son into the world to condemn it, but to save it. There is no eternal doom awaiting those who trust him to save them. But those who don't trust him have already been tried and condemned for not believing in the only Son of God. Their sentence is based on this fact: that the Light from heaven came into the world, but they loved the darkness more than the Light, for their deeds were evil. They hated the heavenly Light because they wanted to sin in the darkness. They stayed away from that Light for fear their sins would be exposed and they would be punished. But those doing right come gladly to the Light to let everyone see that they are doing what God wants them to.

Jesus notes the critical importance of the Holy Spirit, and it is even more in focus today than in previous times. We've already seen many times before the repeated dying and rising cycle that must happen for development and transformation to occur. It is quite interesting that the serpent has a positive connotation in conjunction with both Moses and Jesus here; it truly is one of the great dual symbols in existence, and so the conscious attitude of those confronted with it and the context determine its manifestation. And finally, we have probably the most well-known Gospel verse at John 3:16, which I emboldened, because it shows in full the goodness of God and the light side of the Self.

John 4:10 If only you knew what a wonderful gift God has for you, and who I am, you would ask me for some *living* water!

There is a verse coming shortly where we will note the meaning here.

John 4:14-26 But the water I give them becomes a perpetual spring within them, watering them forever with eternal life... Go and get your husband...All too true. For you have had five husbands, and you aren't even married to the man you're living with now...the time is coming, ma'am, when we will no longer be concerned about whether to worship the Father here or in Jerusalem. For it's not *where* we worship that counts, but *how* we worship-is our worship spiritual and real? Do we have the Holy Spirit's help? For God is Spirit, and we must have his help to worship as we should. The Father wants this kind of worship from us. But you Samaritans know so little about him, worshipping blindly, while we Jews know all about him, for salvation comes to the world through the Jews...(Jesus tells the woman at the well, who believes in the Messiah) I am the Messiah!

Here is the famous episode of the woman at the well, who believes in Jesus and brings many to see him. Yet again, it is an outsider, a very imperfect Samaritan woman, who gets the message. And the character, not the location, of our devotion to the Self is what matters.

John 4:32-38 No, I have some food you don't know about... My nourishment comes from doing the will of God who sent me, and from finishing his work. Do you think the work of harvesting will not begin until the summer ends four months from now? Look around you! Vast fields of human souls are ripening all around us, and are ready now for reaping. The reapers will be paid good wages and will be gathering eternal souls into the granaries of heaven! What joys await the sower and the reaper, both together! For it is true that one sows and someone else reaps. I sent you to reap where you didn't sow; others did the work, and you received the harvest.

The disciples, and indeed all of us, are to sow what we can that fosters individuation while reaping and gathering the fruits of the work towards development and transformation done by those who laid the groundwork, both before us and along with us. We all stand on the shoulders of giants, as it were, and we must never forget that.

John 4:48-50 Won't any of you believe in me unless I do more and more miracles?...Go back home. Your son is healed!

This same issue is raised in the synoptic Gospels...

John 5:6-17 Would you like to get well? (at Bethesda Pool)... Stand up, roll up your sleeping mat and go on home!...Now you are well; don't sin as you did before, or something even worse may happen to you...My Father constantly does good, and I'm following his example (to Jewish leaders criticizing Sabbath healing).

This is the famous healing of the man by the pool at Bethesda, and the question Jesus asks him is critical: do you *want* to be well? How many times do we, as the saying goes, gravitate towards the devil we know instead of what will help us develop and transform? I am guilty of this, and I will bet the reader is as well in certain ways.

This man was surely traumatized and seems to have developed a sense of learned helplessness. He likely developed a self-care system[60] early on, which got him by to a point, but then backfired. Trauma sufferers may become crippled with anxiety, become aggressive, keep away from certain areas of life, turn to drugs/alcohol, and/or develop any number of skewed attitudes in this way. Some may fight, some may flee, and some may freeze (or do some combination of the three)[61]. The way through trauma of any kind is to do what Perseus did with Medusa in the Greek tradition, who was traumatized herself by Athena. With the aid of a mirror (symbolic of seeing our projections and taking them back), he avoids being petrified (double meaning intended) and

---

60.  see D. Kalsched – The Inner World of Trauma as well as Trauma and the Soul
61.  see P. Levine – Waking the Tiger

cuts off her head. Out of the neck come a few things, but the key entity is Pegasus, the winged horse that symbolizes creative energy freed for development and transformation. We must confront our shadows and complexes, no matter how ugly they may be. Only after he accomplishes this can he go to the naked virgin (read: exposed and undeveloped aspects of ourselves) Andromeda, who is chained to rocks, and free her[62], much as Rapunzel was freed from her tower of trauma[63]. Trauma splits us, with the damaged part trapped and left behind and the rest going forward until, like a rubber band stretched too far, we snap and are forced to become whole again.

Jesus is doing good as he says his Father is, which is true, but this does not address the entire nature of God, as we are shortly about to discuss.

John 5:19-47 The Son can do nothing by himself. He does only what he sees the Father doing, and in the same way. For the Father loves the Son, and tells him everything he is doing; and the Son will do far more awesome miracles than this man's healing. He will even raise from the dead anyone he wants to, just as the Father does. And the Father leaves all judgment of sin to his Son, so that everyone will honor the Son, just as they honor the Father. But if you refuse to honor God's son, whom he sent to you, then you are certainly not honoring the Father. I say emphatically that anyone who listens to my message and believes in God who sent me has eternal life, and will never be

---

62. see M. Woodman – Addiction to Perfection
63. see also the predicament of Elsa in the movie *Frozen*. The famous song Let it Go has excellent lyrics in this regard.

damned for his sins, but has already passed out of death into life. And I solemnly declare that the time is coming, in fact, it is here, when the dead shall hear my voice-the voice of the Son of God-and those who listen shall live. The Father has life in himself; and has granted his Son to have life in himself, and to judge the sins of all mankind because he is the Son of Man. Don't be so surprised! Indeed the time is coming when all the dead in their graves shall hear the voice of God's son, and shall rise again-those who have done good, to eternal life; and those who have continued in evil, to judgment. But I pass no judgment without consulting the Father. I judge as I am told. And my judgment is absolutely fair and just, for it is according to the will of God who sent me and is not merely my own. When I make claims about myself they aren't believed, but someone else, yes, John the Baptist, is making these claims for me too. You have gone out to listen to his preaching, and I can assure you that all he says about me is true! But the truest witness I have is not from a man, though I have reminded you about John's witness so that you will believe in me and be saved. John shone brightly for a while, and you benefitted and rejoiced, but I have a greater witness than John. I refer to the miracles I do; these have been assigned me by the Father, and they prove that the Father has sent me. And the Father himself has also testified about me, though not appearing to you personally, or speaking to you directly. But you are not listening to him, for you refuse to believe me-the one sent to you with God's message. You search the Scriptures, for you believe they give you eternal life. And the Scriptures point to me! Yet you won't come to me so that I can give you this life eternal! Your approval or disapproval means nothing to me, for as I know so well, you don't have God's love within you. I know, because I have come to you representing my Father and you refuse to welcome me, though you readily enough receive those who aren't sent from him, but represent only themselves! No wonder you can't believe! For you gladly honor each other, but you don't care about the honor that comes from the only God! Yet it is not I who will accuse you of this to the Father-Moses will! Moses, on whose laws you set your hopes of heaven. For you have refused to believe Moses. He wrote about me, but you refuse to believe him, so you refuse to believe in me. And since you don't believe what he wrote, no wonder you don't believe me either.

This is a bit long-winded, but the Self manifests in many ways and at many times, and we cannot refuse its ultimate authority. Jesus explains this from the Christian perspective here.

John 6:5-12 Philip, where can we buy bread to feed all these people?...Tell everyone to sit down...Now gather the scraps so that nothing is wasted.

John's version of the loaves and fishes miracle...

John 6:26-33 The truth of the matter is that you want to be with me because I fed you, not because you believe in me. But you shouldn't be so concerned about perishable things like food. No, spend your energy seeking the eternal life that I, the Messiah, can give you. For God the Father has sent me for this very purpose...This is the will of God, that you believe in the one he has sent...Moses didn't give it to them. My Father did. And now he offers you true Bread from heaven. The true Bread is a Person-the one sent by God from heaven, and he gives life to the world.

Jesus is the Bread of Life, and we have the same point here that the ego must be secondary to the Self.

John 6:35-70 (Bread of Life Discourse) I am the Bread of Life. No one coming to me will ever be hungry again. Those believing in me will never thirst. But the trouble is, as I have told you before, you haven't believed even though you have seen me. But some will come to me-those the Father has given me-and I will never, never reject them. **For I have come here from heaven to do the will of God who sent me, not to have my own way.** And this is the will of God, that I should not lose even one of all those he has given me, but that I should raise them to eternal life at the Last Day. For it is my Father's will that everyone who sees his Son and believes in him should have eternal life-that I should raise him at the Last Day...Don't murmur among yourselves about my saying that. For no one can come to me unless the Father who sent me draws him to me, and at the Last Day I will cause all such to rise again from the dead. As it is written in the Scriptures, 'They shall all be taught of God.' Those the Father speaks to, who learn the truth from him, will be attracted to me. (Not that anyone actually sees the Father, for only I have seen him.) How earnestly I tell you this-anyone who believes in me already has eternal life! Yes, I am the Bread of Life! When your fathers in the wilderness ate bread from the skies, they all died. But the Bread from heaven gives eternal life to everyone who eats it. I am that Living Bread that came down out of heaven. Anyone eating this Bread shall live forever; this Bread is my flesh given to redeem humanity...With all the earnestness I possess I tell you this: **Unless you eat the flesh of the Messiah and drink his blood, you cannot have eternal life within you.** But anyone who does eat my flesh and drink my blood has eternal life, and I will raise him at the Last Day. For my flesh is the true food, and my blood is the true drink. **Everyone who eats my flesh and drinks my blood is in me, and I in him.** I live by the power of the living Father who sent me, and in the same way those who partake of me shall live because of me! I am the true Bread from heaven; and anyone who eats this Bread shall live forever, and not die as your fathers did-though they ate bread from heaven...Does *this* offend you? Then what will you think if you see me, the Messiah, return to heaven again? Only the Holy Spirit gives eternal life. Those born only once, with physical birth, will never receive this gift. But now I have told you how to get this true spiritual life. But some of you don't believe me...That is what I meant when I said that no one can come to me unless the Father attracts him to me... (to the Twelve) Are you going (away) too?...I chose the twelve of you, and one is a devil (Judas).

There are two major points from the Bread of Life Discourse that I want to mention. One is the repeated theme of the Self being primary compared to the ego. The other is the way we become one with God through the flesh and blood of the Son. I would rather not argue about whether or not this is to be taken literally because that discussion is not only off the mark but has led to great division among Christians, and as we saw, a house divided cannot stand. The meaning is what matters, and that is to follow our individuation processes, which will eventually lead to the development and transformation, borne out of connection to and partaking in the Self, that makes a unity of reality[64].

---

64. As Jung notes, those in the Eastern traditions believe that one actually becomes the god. See C.G. Jung – Jung on Ignatius of Loyola's Spiritual Exercises.

John 7:6-8 It is not the right time for me to go now. But you can go anytime and it will make no difference, for the world can't hate you; but it does hate me, because I accuse it of sin and evil. You go on, and I'll come later when it is the right time.

It is not yet Jesus' time...

John 7:16-24 I'm not teaching you my own thoughts, but those of God who sent me. If any of you really determines to do God's will, then you will certainly know whether my teaching is from God or is merely my own. Anyone presenting his own ideas is looking for praise for himself, but anyone seeking to honor the one who sent him is a good and true person. None of you obeys the laws of Moses! So why pick on me for breaking them? Why kill me for this!...I worked on the Sabbath by healing a man, and you were surprised. But you work on the Sabbath, too, whenever you obey Moses' law of circumcision (actually, however, this tradition of circumcision is older than the Mosaic law); for if the correct time for circumcising your children falls on the Sabbath, you go ahead and do it, as you should. So why should I be condemned for making a man completely well on the Sabbath? Think this through and you will see that I am right.

Again, Jesus has no time for human-made rules and laws. The Sabbath is for humans, not the other way around.

John 7:28-29 Yes, you know me and where I was born and raised, but I am the representative of one you don't know, and he is Truth. I know him because I was with him, and he sent me to you.

Pretty direct meaning here...

John 7:33-34 [Not yet!] I am to be here a little longer. Then I shall return to the one who sent me. You will search for me but not find me. And you won't be able to come where I am!

Jesus' time has not yet come...

John 7:37-38 If anyone is thirsty, let him come to me and drink. For the Scriptures declare that rivers of living water shall flow from the inmost being of anyone who believes in me.

The living water, or the *aqua permanens* in alchemy, arises ultimately out of the Self and can be transferred to us if we maintain a healthy connection to the Self.

John 8:7-11 All right, hurl the stones at her until she dies. But only he who never sinned may throw the first! (Jesus writes in the dust/sand)...Where are your accusers? Didn't even one of them condemn you?...Neither do I. Go and sin no more.

This is the famous episode where Jesus tells anyone without sin to cast the first stone at this woman who committed adultery, and of course no one does. Again, God cares about what you do, but God cares about transformation more. Jesus, I believe, is writing her story in the sands of time[65], as it were, to be an eternal example for all.

John 8:12-29 I am the Light of the world. So if you follow me, you won't be stumbling through the darkness, for living light will flood your path...These claims are true even though I make them concerning myself. For I know where I came from and where I am going, but you don't know this about me. You pass judgment on me without knowing the facts. I am not judging you now; but if I were, it would be an absolutely correct judgment in every respect, for I have with me the Father who sent me. Your laws

---

65.   There is a clear parallel, via a story written in the wind, from DragonForce – The Last Dragonborn.

say that if two men agree on something that has happened, their witness is accepted as fact. Well, I am one witness, and my Father who sent me I the other....You don't know who I am, so you don't know who my Father is. If you knew me, then you would know him too...I am going away; and you will search for me, and die in your sins. And you cannot come where I am going...You are from below; I am from above. You are of this world; I am not. That is why I said that you will die in your sins; for unless you believe that I am the Messiah, the Son of God, you will die in your sins...I am the one I have always claimed to be. I could condemn you for much and teach you much, but I won't, for I say only what I am told to by the one who sent me; and he is Truth...When you have killed the Messiah, then you will realize that I am he and that I have not been telling you my own ideas, but have spoken what the Father taught me. And he who sent me is with me-he has not deserted me-for I always do those things that are pleasing to him.

The Self brings the light of conscious awareness that leads to development and transformation.

John 8:31-32 You are truly my disciples if you live as I tell you to, **and you will know the truth, and the truth will set you free.**

One of the most famous and important Gospel passages. The meaning is obvious, but can we accept the *whole* truth?

John 8:34-58 You are slaves of sin, every one of you. And slaves don't have rights, but the Son has every right there is! So if the Son sets you free, you will indeed be free-(Yes, I realize that you are descendants of Abraham!) And yet some of you are trying to kill me because my message does not find a home within your hearts. I am telling you what I saw when I was with my Father. But you are following the advice of your father...No! For if he were, you would follow his good example (Abraham is not their father). But instead you are trying to kill me-and all because I told you the truth I heard from God. Abraham wouldn't do a thing like that! No, you are obeying your real father when you act that way...If that were so, then you would love me, for I have come to you from God. I am not here on my own, but he sent me. Why can't you understand what I am saying? It is because you are prevented from doing so! For you are the children of your father the devil and you love to do the evil things he does. He was a murderer from the beginning and a hater of truth-there is not an iota of truth in him. When he lies, it is perfectly normal; for he is the father of liars. And so when I tell the truth, you just naturally don't believe it! Which of you can truthfully accuse me of one single sin? [No one!] And since I am telling you the truth, why don't you believe me? Anyone whose Father is God listens gladly to the words of God. Since you don't, it proves you aren't his children... No. I have no demon in me. For I honor my Father-and you dishonor me. And though I have no wish to make myself great, God wants this for me and judges [those who reject me]. With all the earnestness I have I tell you this-no one who obeys me shall ever die!...If I am merely boasting about myself, it doesn't count. But it is my Father-and you claim him as your God-who is saying these glorious things about me. But you do not even know him. I do. If I said otherwise, I would be as great a liar as you! But it is true-I know him and fully obey him. Your father Abraham rejoiced to see my day. He knew I was coming and was glad...The absolute truth is that I was in existence before Abraham was ever born!

The main point here is that we are all slaves to something, be it money, substances, gambling, food, attitudes, ways of life, or any number of other areas. These demons, ultimately reflecting our shadows and complexes, must be confronted and transformed.

John 9:3-7 Neither (regarding a question about if the blind man was blind due to sin or due to parents). But to demonstrate the power of God. All of us must quickly carry out the tasks assigned us by the one who sent me, for there is little time left before the night falls and all work comes to an end. But while I am still here in the world, I give it my light...Go and wash in the Pool of Siloam.

Problems are usually a combination of factors, and there is always much work to be done regarding developing the light of consciousness and following the Self. The other aspects of this passage will be discussed momentarily regarding why such issues occur.

John 9:35-41 Do you believe in the Messiah...you have seen him, and he is speaking to you!...I have come into the world to give sight to those who are spiritually blind and to show those who think they see that they are blind...If you were blind, you wouldn't be guilty. But your guilt remains because you claim to know what you are doing.

Jesus comes to bring conscious awareness for those who have eyes to see and ears to hear, and those people are often the metaphorical stones that the builders reject. One may not be guilty for being unaware, but *not knowing functions like guilt in the eyes of nature.* Those who think they know everything and are certain they are acting correctly are too often frauds; their hubris is like that of Icarus in the Greek tradition, who gets so inflated that he flies too close to the sun, which burns his wings and sends him crashing to the ground[66].

John 10:1-38 Anyone refusing to walk through the gate into a sheepfold, who sneaks over the wall, must surely be a thief! For a shepherd comes through the gate. The gatekeeper opens the gate for him, and the sheep hear his voice and come to him; and he calls his own sheep by name and leads them out. He walks ahead of them; and they follow him, for they recognize his voice. They won't follow a stranger but will run from him, for they don't recognize his voice...I am the Gate for the sheep. All others who came before me were thieves and robbers. But the true sheep did not listen to them. Yes, I am the Gate. Those who come in by way of the Gate will be saved and will go in and out and find green pastures. **The thief's purpose is to steal, kill and destroy. My purpose is to give life in all its fullness.** I am the Good shepherd. The Good Shepherd lays down his life for the sheep. A hired man will run when he sees a wolf coming and will leave the sheep, for they aren't his and he isn't their shepherd. And so the wolf leaps on them and scatters the flock. The hired man runs because he is hired and has no real concern for the sheep. I am the Good shepherd and know my own sheep, and they know me, just as my Father knows me and I know the Father; and I lay down my life for the sheep. I have other sheep, too, in another fold. I must bring them also, and they will heed my voice; and there will be one flock with one Shepherd. The Father loves me because I lay down

---

66.   see E.F. Edinger – The Eternal Drama: The Inner Meaning of Greek Mythology

my life that I may have it back again. No one can kill me without my consent-I lay down my life voluntarily. For I have the right and power to lay it down when I want to and also the right and power to take it again. For the Father has given me this right...I have already told you, and you don't believe me. The proof is in the miracles I do in the name of my Father. But you don't believe me because you are not part of my flock. My sheep recognize my voice, and I know them, and they follow me. I give them eternal life and they shall never perish. No one shall snatch them away from me, for my Father has given them to me, and he is more powerful than anyone else, so no one can kidnap them from me. I and the Father are one...At God's direction I have done many a miracle to help the people. For which one are you killing me?... In your own Law it says that **men are gods!** So if the Scripture, which cannot be untrue, speaks of those as gods to whom the message of God came, do you call it blasphemy when the one sanctified and sent into the world by the Father says, 'I am the Son of God'? Don't believe me unless I do miracles of God. But if I do, believe them even if you don't believe me. Then you will become convinced that the Father is in me, and I in the Father.

I have emboldened the section that I did because it is a very strong pro-life statement by Jesus himself. Biology backs him up, as life is defined as beginning at conception and persisting until natural death[67]. People who are pro-life are not pro-

67. The United States Supreme Court abolished Roe v. Wade, which never should have existed in the first place according to people on both sides of the aisle, at exactly 10:10 AM, and the emboldened verse above regarding life is John 10:10. This was absolutely intentional; of that there can be no doubt. See also Proverbs 24:11-12.

birth only, as Jesus and they both care for those in need at any point throughout the lifespan. I'm not going to engage in any arguments in this area, as the matter is not up for debate, and it would lead us way too far astray. *But no development or transformation can occur without life in the space-time frame, and that is the purpose, achieved by conscious awareness, of each of our lives.* The issue is not at all political or religious, even though people try to make it that way. No human created the ability for life, and so no human has the right to take it away or to define what it means. And without your life, you can have no opinion or view at all, a point that the great Ronald Reagan made when he noted that everyone who is pro-choice has "already been born." The choice is before the act, not after the fact. Abortion is a crime against nature, the universe, etc[68]. Of course, the meaning of this section is psychological as well; Jesus wants us to live our lives fully (thriving and not just surviving). This can be a major challenge, but it means we have to go into the areas of ourselves, guided by the Self, that we do not like, in order to have that more abundant, complete life. If we are gods, as Jesus explicitly mentions here, then we must be the faithful but not blind sheep, who by entering the fold via the narrow gate, as the

---

68.  In The Aion Lectures, E.F. Edinger explicitly states this is the case regarding abortion as a crime against nature, the universe, etc. He then hedges his statement, for reasons very suspectible but unknown, by saying that it is not a black and white issue. Just like action potentials are all-or-nothing phenomena or, alternatively, something like the Pauli Exclusion Principle, some things, though not many, are black and white in life. I therefore vehemently challenge this hedging except in cases of threat to the life of the mother. Any other position violates his own statement and the discussion above as well as nature itself.

great alchemist Morienus reminded us earlier, move towards development, transformation, and individuation.

John 11:4 The purpose of his illness is not death, but for the glory of God. I, the Son of God, will receive glory from this situation.

Nature imposes illnesses of many types for the purpose of development and transformation, which, if realized, brings glory to both human and divine. It is a two-way evolutionary street, and we are just about to see why this is the case.

John 11:7-44 Let's go to Judea...There are twelve hours of daylight every day, and during every hour of it a man can walk safely and not stumble. Only at night is there danger of a wrong step, because of the dark. Our friend Lazarus has gone to sleep, but now I will go and waken him!...Lazarus is dead. And for your sake, I am glad I wasn't there, for this will give you another opportunity to believe in me. Come, let's go to him...Your brother will come back to life again...I am the one who raises the dead and gives them life again. Anyone who believes in me, even though he dies like anyone else, shall live again. He is given eternal life for believing in me and shall never perish. Do you believe this, Martha?...Where is he buried?...Roll the stone aside...But didn't I tell you that you will see a wonderful miracle from God if you believe?...Father, thank you for hearing me. (You always hear me, of course, but I said it because of all these people standing here, so that they will believe you sent me.). Lazarus, come out!... Unwrap him and let him go!

Darkness, or lack of awareness and fidelity to the Self, is indeed the stumbling block. Here we have one of Jesus' greatest miracles, the raising of Lazarus from the dead. How many of us are psychologically "dead," as it were, and in need of rebirth on a new level?

John 12:7-8 Let her alone. She did it in preparation for my burial. You can always help the poor, but I won't be with you very long.

This has the same meaning as discussed in the three synoptic Gospels, where this exact anointing is mentioned.

John 12:23-50 I must fall and die like a kernel of wheat that falls into the furrows of the earth. Unless I die I will be alone-a single seed. But my death will produce many new wheat kernels-a plentiful harvest of new lives. If you love your life down here-you will lose it. If you despise your life down here-you will exchange it for eternal glory. If these Greeks want to be my disciples, tell them to come and follow me, for my servants must be where I am. And if they follow me, the Father will honor them. Now my soul is deeply troubled. Shall I pray, 'Father, save me from what lies ahead'? But that is the very reason why I came! Father, bring glory and honor to your name...The voice was for your benefit, not mine. The time of judgment for the world has come-and the time when Satan, the prince of this world, shall be cast out. And when I am lifted up [on the cross], I will draw everyone to me... My light will shine out for you just a little while longer. Walk in it while you can, and go where you want to go before the darkness falls, for then it will be too late for you to find your way. Make use of the Light while there is still time, then you will become light bearers...If you trust me, you are really trusting God. For when you see me, you are seeing the one who sent me. I have come as a Light to shine in this dark world, so that all who put their trust in me will no longer wander in the darkness. If anyone hears me and doesn't obey me, I am not his judge-for I have come to save the world and not to judge it. But all who reject me and my message will be judged at the Day of Judgment by the truths I have spoken. For these are not my own ideas, but I have told you what the Father said to tell you. And I know his instructions lead to eternal life; so whatever he tells me to say, I say!

Jesus discusses his impending death and resurrection and the fact that his individuation process must take place above all else. We are to do the same according to our own identities and purposes. The light of consciousness and the willingness to bear one's cross is of the utmost importance.

John 13:7-38 You don't understand now why I am doing it; some day you will...But if I don't (to Peter), you can't be my partner... One who has bathed all over needs only to have his feet washed to be entirely clean. Now you are clean-but that isn't true of everyone here...Not all of you are clean...Do you understand what I was doing? You call me 'Master' and 'Lord,' and you do well to say it, for it is true. And since I, the Lord and Teacher, have washed your feet, you ought to wash each other's feet. I have given you an example to follow: do as I have done to you. How true it is that a servant is not greater than his master. Nor is the messenger more important than the one who sends him. You know these things-now do them! That is the path of blessing. I am not saying these things to all of you; I know so well each one of you I chose. The Scripture declares, 'One who eats supper with me will betray me,' and this will soon come true. I tell you this now so that when it happens, you will believe in me. Truly, anyone welcoming my messenger is welcoming me. And to welcome me is to welcome the Father who sent me...Yes, it is true-one of you will betray me...It is the one I honor by giving the bread dipped in the sauce...Hurry-do it now...My time has come; the glory of God will soon surround me-and God shall receive great praise because of all that happens to me. And God shall give me his own glory; and this so very soon. Dear, dear children, how brief are these moments before I must go away and leave you! Then, though you search for me, you cannot come to me-just as I told the Jewish leaders. And so I am giving a new commandment to you now-love each other just as much as I love you. Your strong love for each other will prove to the world that you are my disciples...You can't go with me now; but you will follow me later...Die for me? No-three times before the cock crows tomorrow morning, you will deny that you even know me (to Peter)!

Jesus talks about his passion and things that will occur, including yet again the denials of Peter. But the key is the command to love God and love one another. If love isn't present, power predominates and spoils development and transformation.

John 14:1-31 Let not your heart be troubled. You are trusting God, now trust in me. There are many homes up there where my Father lives, and I am going to prepare them for your coming. When everything is ready, then I will come and get you, so that you can always be with me where I am. If this weren't so, I would tell you plainly. And you know where I am going and how to get there...**I am the Way-yes, and the Truth and the Life**. No one can get to the Father except by means of me. If you had known who I am, then you would have known who my Father is. From now on you know him-and have seen him!...Don't you even yet know who I am, Philip, even after all this time I have been with you? Anyone who has seen me has seen the Father! So why are you asking to see him? Don't you believe that I am in the Father and the Father is in me? The words I say are not my own but are from my Father who lives in me. And he does his work through me. Just believe it-that I am in the Father and the Father is in me. Or else believe it because of the mighty miracles you have seen me do. **In solemn truth I tell you, anyone believing in me shall do the same miracles I have done, and even greater ones, because I am going to be with the Father.** You can ask him for *anything*, using my name, and I will do it, for this will bring praise to the Father because of what I, the Son, will do for you. Yes, ask *anything*, using my name, and I will do it! If you love me, obey me; and I will ask the Father and he will give you another Comforter, and he will never leave you. He is the Holy Spirit, the Spirit who leads into all truth. The world at large cannot receive him, for it isn't looking for him and doesn't recognize him. But you do, for he lives with you now and someday shall be in you. No, I will not abandon you or leave you as orphans in the storm-I will come to you. In just a little while I will be gone from the world, but I will still be present with you. For I will live again-and you will too. When I come back to life again, you will know that I am in my Father, and you in me, and I in you. The one who obeys me is the one who loves me; and because he loves me, my Father will love him; and I will too, and I will reveal myself to him...Because I will only reveal myself to those who love me and obey me. The Father will love them too, and we will come to them and live with them. Anyone who doesn't obey me doesn't love me. And remember, I am not making up this answer to your question! It is the answer given by the Father who sent me. I am telling you these things now while I am still with you. But when the Father sends the Comforter instead of me-and by the Comforter I mean the Holy Spirit-he will teach you much, as well as remind you of everything I myself have told you. I am leaving you with a gift-peace of mind and heart! And the peace I give isn't fragile like the peace the world gives. So don't be troubled or afraid. Remember what I told you-I am going away, but I will come back to you again. If you really love me, you will be very happy for me, for now I can go to the Father, who is greater than I am. I have told you these things before they happen so that when they do, you will believe [in me]. I don't have much more time to talk to you, for the evil prince of this world approaches. He has no power over me, but I will freely do what the Father requires of me so that the world will know that I love the Father. Come, let's be going.

Jesus tells us not to worry and that there are many rooms prepared, likely according to our state of development and transformation, our personalities, etc., for us in the state of being we call Heaven. Jesus notes that he is the Way, the Truth, and the Life, which he is from the Christian perspective. But this is a dangerous verse if taken literally, because that makes everyone else's deity invalid and both can and has led to war. Jesus is a symbol of the Self for Christians, and as we have stated, the Self is the way to the states we call Heaven, Nirvana, etc. It is universal and both includes and transcends all imagery from all spiritual backgrounds. Jesus also speaks at great length about the Holy Spirit, and that form of God is more relevant than ever today from the Christian perspective as it is within and around each of us, ready to help drive development, transformation, and individuation.

I emboldened the critically important passages, including John 14:12, because they finally allow us to make sense of the key points about God and our relationship with God. But we need to return to the Old Testament for a moment for more context, back to the Book of Job. Here is a summary of the story:

Yahweh makes an explicitly stated bet with Satan in the Book of Job that his servant Job will remain faithful even in the face of extreme hardship. Yahweh then proceeds to inflict great suffering upon Job, who is advised by his friends to submit and give up his fight. But Job refuses to retract his demand for a fair trial before the Deity, and Yahweh even acknowledges this right, but not before taking nearly literally everything Job has and crippling or destroying it. Eventually Yahweh restores what Job had with new people and things, but touts his own great power in the process.

There are numerous problems with Yahweh's actions here. Making a bet with what we might interpret as the dark side of himself, or the dark son to the light Jesus in some versions/ interpretations, is inherently problematic for obvious reasons. Job, being mortal, has no chance against an immortal being. While it is true that Job had a narcissism issue, the punishment clearly does not fit the crime if one reads the Book of Job. From a Jungian perspective, Job was actually morally superior to Yahweh due to his higher level of activated conscious awareness. Had Yahweh consulted his omniscience instead of remaining unconscious in this area, the whole episode could have been prevented[69]. These are not the actions of either a loving parent or a loving God, and this was so much the case that Yahweh was forced to provide an "answer to Job," which meant he had to incarnate as Jesus to set things right between human and divine. This opened the door for two-way or bidirectional development and transformation of humans and God. In other words, *we need God and God needs us.*

Interestingly, Yahweh has at times even directly indicated that he has a dark side!

Then the Lord said to Moses, "Go to Pharaoh, for I have made him and his servants obdurate in order that I may perform these signs of mine among them and that you may recount to your son and grandson how ruthlessly I dealt with the Egyptians and what signs I wrought among them, so that you may know that I am the Lord. (Exodus 10:1-2)

I am the Lord, there is no other; I form the light, and create the darkness, I make well-being and create woe; I the Lord do all these things. (Isaiah 45:6-7)

John 1:2-5, as we just saw, states explicitly that God created everything, and we all know both dark and light exist, so there is no way to spin that passage except that God is ultimately responsible for the creation of all aspects of reality. And since we are made in the image and likeness of God, we need only to realize the opposites in ourselves to infer their existence in God, not to mention it is explicitly stated in various places as well. And Job isn't the only example. Yahweh flooding the entire earth and killing nearly everything in the process is an act he

---

69.   see C.G. Jung – Answer to Job (CW 11)

explicitly apologizes for doing. Jacob wrestles with the angel, and even though he suffers a broken hip in the struggle, he forces the angel to bless him. The examples are numerous, and in the Book of Revelation there is even a "wrathful Lamb" side of Jesus that is evident.

The terrible fact about Yahweh is that he uses a nation or an individual as an agent of his divine wrath, a vessel to pour out his punishing wrath on someone else, and then he holds that agent personally responsible for the actions that he, Yahweh, had made him do! That is explicit here, absolutely explicit. And it is psychologically true too. (E.F. Edinger)[70]

In certain cases, this issue is of such importance that it takes on the urgency of a life or death situation. That means the ultimate archetypal projections are often activated: God and the devil, two sides of the same phenomenon. (E.F. Edinger)[71]

Job expects that God will, in a sense, stand by him against God; in this we have a picture of God's tragic contradictoriness. This was the main theme of *Answer to Job*. (C.G. Jung)[72]

The "relativity of God," as I understand it, denotes a point of view that does not conceive of God as "absolute," i.e., wholly "cut off" from man and existing outside and beyond all human conditions, but as in a certain sense dependent on him; it also

---

70.   from E.F. Edinger – Ego and Self: The Old Testament Prophets, p. 66
71.   E.F Edinger – The Mysterium Lectures (p. 316)
72.   C.G. Jung – Memories, Dreams, Reflections – p. 216; also recall Meister Eckhart's prayer for God's help against God, something of which Jacob Boehme also was aware. Eckhart and Boehme are the two most cited mystics by Jung.

implies a reciprocal and essential relation between man and God, whereby man can be understood as a function of God, and God as a psychological function of man. (C.G. Jung)[73]

Only here, in life on earth, where the opposites clash together, can the general level of consciousness be raised. (C.G. Jung)[74]

Their sin was that they refused to show God the way,
and this suggests that God needs man to help him.
He asks man to be the instrument for reaching higher
consciousness. In the mystical sense this means that the human
psyche is the place where God can become conscious.
(M-L. Von Franz)[75]

Psychologically the case is clear, since the dogmatic figure of Christ is so sublime and spotless that everything else turns dark beside it. It is, in fact, so one-sidedly perfect that it demands a psychic complement to restore the balance. This inevitable opposition led very early to the doctrine of the two sons of God, of whom the elder was called Satanael. The coming of the Antichrist is not just a prophetic prediction – it is an inexorable psychological law whose existence, though unknown to the author of the Johannine Epistles, brought him a sure knowledge of the impending enantiodromia.
(C.G. Jung)[76]

One of these revelations is the Holy Ghost.
As a being who existed before the world was, he is eternal,

---

73.   C.G. Jung – Psychological Types [CW 6, para. 412, p. 243]
74.   from C.G. Jung – Memories, Dreams, Reflections, p. 311
75.   from M-L. Von Franz - The interpretation of Fairy Tales (Rev. ed.), p. 194
76.   C.G. Jung – Aion [CW 9(II), para. 77, p. 42-43]

but he appears empirically in this world only when
Christ had left the earthly stage. He will be for the disciples
what Christ was for them. He will invest them with the power
to do works greater, perhaps, than those of the Son.

(C.G. Jung)[77]

Jung directly mentions the key passage at John 14:12 here. *The
greater works than even Jesus did that Jesus himself said we must
do involve us developing and transforming ourselves in context of
the Self as we move towards individuation. This in turn affects
everyone and everything around and within us, including God.*
The observer affects the observed, so quantum physics backs
this up in addition to Jungian-based psychology. Hinduism
(*Atman*) and Buddhism (*Tao*) have the notion of a dual-natured
deity built in. There is only one Force in Star Wars, with a light
and a dark side, not two Forces. If one simply looks around,
there are beautiful people, animals, and landscapes, but there
are also horrible forces of nature that, for example, create
hurricanes that wipe out entire areas and kill hundreds of
people, and nature itself is set up where living things eat other
living things. No entity except an archetypal (divine) one could
create such phenomena. Jesus calls God the Father good, but
those statements do not exclude the bad. If you have a stove
with four burners and two are on while two are off, it is correct,
but not completely so, to say the stove is hot. Hot makes no
sense without cold, up makes no sense without down, and good
makes no sense without evil. Nothing makes any sense without
its opposite; there is no reference point otherwise.

---

77.   C.G. Jung – Psychology and Religion [CW 11, para. 204, p. 135]

The data is very clear on this point, whether explicit (East) or forced into the unconscious but still directly there (West). *God is a unity and cannot be broken into pieces*[78]! This awareness and the work it entails are tasks yet to be completed and fall into the bidirectional transformative process between humans and God.

> If the God grows old, he becomes shadow, nonsense, and he goes down. The greatest truth becomes the greatest lie, the brightest day becomes darkest night. (C.G. Jung)[79]

If one reads the Bible, it is immediately evident that Jesus is a clearly evolved God compared to Yahweh, and more subtly evident that the Holy Spirit is an evolved God compared to Jesus because it unites and transcends all opposites. Anything that stagnates dies, so this evolution is necessary for the *living* God from the Christian perspective. According to the data, we play a critical role in these processes[80]. As Jesus requested, we ask God not to lead us into temptation in the Our Father, which is reasonable, but why is this necessary in the first place if God consisted of only light and no dark?

> We do not know whether there is more good than evil or whether the good is stronger. We can only hope that the good will predominate. If good is identified with constructiveness, there is some probability that life will go on in a more or less endurable form; but if the destructive were to prevail, the

---

78. D. Bohm developed a theory of quantum physics that treats the nature of reality and the entirety of existence as an unfragmented whole; this is the idea behind the concept of *implicate order*. The Cosmic Self/God would entail the whole of reality by definition.
79. from C.G. Jung – Liber Novus (The Red Book), p. 242
80. The discovery of extraterrestrial life forms does not/will not change anything we have discussed; we still have the capacities we do. It might knock human narcissism down a few pegs though!

world would surely have done itself to death long ago....Hence the optimistic assumption of psychotherapy that conscious realization accentuates the good more than overshadowing evil. Becoming conscious reconciles the opposites and thus creates a higher third. (C.G. Jung)[81]

Put very succinctly:

Whoever knows God has an effect on Him.

(C.G. Jung)[82]

The difference between humans and God is one of completeness and the nature of the opposites. We are infinitesimally small (ego) compared to God (Self) and far less complete. The storm of opposites rages in each of us, but God is a transcendence of the opposites into a higher third at a far greater level than is found within us, resulting in more peace overall[83]. No one is trying to raise humans to the level of God in this book, but rather to point out the bidirectional transformations that take place. It is a positive inflation to think one (ego) is higher than God (Self), but a negative inflation to think one has nothing to offer God and that humans are solely responsible for everything dark. Neither is true, and both are bad.

Further, some may argue that if God has a dark side, then that is some kind of justification for bad behavior by humans because of the image and likeness issue. Nothing could be further from the truth; it is our collective purpose to create consciousness for the goal of development and transformation[84], not to be destructive because

---

81. as cited in M-L. Von Franz - Psychotherapy
82. from C.G. Jung – Answer to Job [CW 11, para. 617, p. 391]
83. see C.G. Jung – Jung on Ignatius of Loyola's Spiritual Exercises
84. see E.F. Edinger – The Creation of Consciousness; free will is directly proportional to the level of conscious awareness.

we can't help it. But now we can see how everything ties together, as well as why God gravitates towards the sick and the outsiders (both to help them and for self-transformation). Jesus refers to himself as the Son of Man numerous times in the Gospels, and based on the above, we indeed give birth to a transformed and evolved God.

John 15:1-27 I am the true Vine, and my Father is the Gardener. He lops off every branch that doesn't produce. And he prunes those branches that bear fruit for even larger crops. He has already tended you by pruning you back for greater strength and usefulness by means of the commands I gave you. Take care to live in me, and let me live in you. For a branch can't produce fruit when severed from the vine. Nor can you be fruitful apart from me. **Yes, I am the Vine; you are the branches. Whoever lives in me and I in him shall produce a large crop of fruit. For apart from me you can't do a thing.** If anyone separates from me, he is thrown away like a useless branch, withers, and is gathered into a pile with all the others and burned. But if you stay in me and obey my commands, you may ask any request you like, and it will be granted! My true disciples produce bountiful harvests. This brings great glory to my Father. I have loved you even as the Father has loved me. Live within my love. When you obey me you are living in my love, just as I obey my Father and live in his love. I have told you this so that you will be filled with my joy. Yes, your cup of joy will overflow! I demand that you love each other as much as I love you. And here is how to measure it-the greatest love is shown when a person lays down his life for his friends; and you are my friends if you obey me. I no longer call you slaves, for a master doesn't confide in his slaves; now you are my friends, proved by the fact that I have told you everything the

Father told me. You didn't choose me! I chose you! I appointed you to go and produce lovely fruit always, so that no matter what you ask for from the Father, using my name, he will give it to you. I demand that you love each other, for you get enough hate from the world! But then, it hated me before it hated you. The world would love you if you belonged to it; but you don't-for I chose you to come out of the world, and so it hates you. Do you remember what I told you? 'A slave isn't greater than his master!' So since they persecuted me, naturally they will persecute you. And if they had listened to me, they would listen to you! The people of the world will persecute you because you belong to me, for they don't know God who sent me. They would not be guilty if I had not come and spoken to them. But now they have no excuse for their sin. Anyone hating me is also hating my Father. If I hadn't done such mighty miracles among them they would not be counted guilty. But as it is, they saw these miracles and yet they hated both of us-me and my Father. This has fulfilled what the prophets said concerning the Messiah, 'They hated me without reason.' But I will send you the Comforter-the Holy Spirit, the source of all truth. He will come to you from the Father and will tell you all about me. And you also must tell everyone about me, because you have been with me from the beginning.

This famous passage about the Vine and the branches is a perfect description of the ego-Self axis. Without connection to the Self we indeed can do nothing. Jesus elevates anyone who follows him in this section to the level of "friend," and that is accurate regarding how development and transformation occur: it is a *co-creative process*, and we are all on the same team, as it were. And this is for all, so it is our duty to tell people about the Self, but in terms of the God-images that apply to them, not necessarily those that apply to us. This forcing of a certain God-image is the great error of evangelism as traditionally understood.

John 16:1-33 I have told you these things so that you won't be staggered [by all that lies ahead.] For you will be excommunicated from the synagogues, and indeed the time is coming when those who kill you will think they are doing God a service. This is because they have never known the Father or me. Yes, I'm telling you these things now so that when they happen you will remember I warned you. I didn't tell you earlier because I was going to be with you for a while longer. But now I am going away to the one who sent me, and none of you seems interested in the purpose of my going; none wonders why. Instead you are only filled with sorrow. But the fact of the matter is that it is best for you that I go away, for if I don't, the Comforter won't come. If I do, he will-for I will send him to you. And when he has come he will convince the world of its sin, and of the availability of God's goodness, and of deliverance from judgment. The world's sin is unbelief in me; there is righteousness available because I go to the Father and you shall see me no more; there is deliverance from judgment because the prince of this world has already been judged. **Oh, there is so much more I want to tell you, but you can't understand it now.** When the Holy spirit, who is truth, comes, he shall guide you into all truth, for he will not be presenting his own ideas, but will be passing on to you what he has heard. He will tell you about the future. He shall praise me and bring me great honor by showing you my glory. All the Father's glory is mine; this is what I mean when I say that he will show you my glory. In just a little while I will be gone, and you will see me no more; but just a little while after that, and you will see me again!...Are you asking yourselves what I mean? The world will greatly rejoice over what is going to happen to me, and you will weep. But your weeping shall suddenly be turned to wonderful joy [when you see me again]. It will be the same joy as that of a woman in labor when her child is born-her anguish gives place to rapturous joy and the pain is forgotten. You have sorrow now, but I will see you again and then you will rejoice; and no one can rob you of that joy. At that time you won't need to ask me for anything, for you can go directly to the Father and ask him, and he will give you what you ask for because you use my name. You haven't tried this before, [but begin now]. Ask, using my name, and you will receive, and your cup of joy will overflow.

I have spoken of these matters very guardedly, but the time will come when this will not be necessary and I will tell you plainly all about the Father. Then you will present your petitions over my signature! And I won't need to ask the Father to grant you these requests, for the Father himself loves you dearly because you love me and believe that I came from the Father. Yes, I came from the Father into the world and will leave the world and return to the Father...Do you finally believe this? But the time is coming-in fact, it is here-when you will be scattered, each one returning to his own home, leaving me alone. Yet I will not be alone, for the Father is with me. I have told you all this so that you will have peace of heart and mind. **Here on earth you will have many trials and sorrows; but cheer up, for I have overcome the world.**

Jesus notes the coming evolution of the Godhead into the form of the Holy Spirit and the state of sinfulness that is disconnect from the Self. He explains why he speaks in parables and leaves the truth to be discovered at the right moments by those who have developed eyes to see and ears to hear. Jesus overcomes the world, and if the pattern for our lives is the Self, we can accomplish that as well by activating the hero function within[85].

John 17:1-26 Father, the time has come. Reveal the glory of your Son so that he can give the glory back to you. For you have given him authority over every man and woman in all the earth. He gives eternal life to each one you have given him. And this is the way to have eternal life-by knowing you, the only true God, and Jesus Christ, the one you sent to earth! I brought glory to you here on earth by doing everything you told me to. And now, Father, reveal my glory as I stand in your presence, the glory we shared before the world began. I have told these men all about you. They were in the world, but then you gave them to me. Actually, they were always yours, and you gave them to me; and they have obeyed you. Now they know that everything I have is a gift from you, for I have passed on to them the commands you gave me; and they accepted them and know of a certainty that I came down to earth from you, and they believe you sent me. My plea is not for the world but for those you have given me because they belong to you. And all of them, since they are mine, belong to you; and you have given them back to me with everything else of yours, and so *they are my glory!* Now I am leaving the world, and leaving them behind, and coming to you. Holy Father, keep them in your own care-all those you have given me-so that they will be united just as we are, with none missing. During my time here I have kept safe within your

---

85.    see J. Campbell – The Hero with a Thousand Faces

family all of these you gave me. I guarded them so that not one perished, except the son of hell, as the Scriptures foretold. And now I am coming to you. I have told them many things while I was with them so that they would be filled with my joy. I have given them your commands. And the world hates them because they don't fit in with it, just as I don't. I'm not asking you to take them out of the world, but to keep them safe from Satan's power. They aren't part of this world any more than I am. Make them pure and holy through teaching them your words of truth. As you sent me into the world, I am sending them into the world, and I consecrate myself to meet their need for growth in truth and holiness. I am not praying for these alone but also for the future believers who will come to me because of the testimony of these. My prayer for all of them is that they will be of one heart and mind, just as you and I are. Father-that just as you are in me and I am in you, so they will be in us, and the world will believe you sent me. I have given them the glory you gave me-the glorious unity of being one, as we are-I in them and you in me, all being perfected into one- so that the world will know you sent me and will understand that you love them as much as you love me. Father, I want them with me-these you've given me-so that they can see my glory. You gave me the glory because you loved me before the world began! O righteous Father, the world doesn't know you, but I do; and these disciples know you sent me. And I have revealed you to them, and will keep on revealing you so that the mighty love you have for me may be in them, and I in them.

Jesus prays for us here and makes clear the importance of individuation and union with the Self. The note about Satan perishing and protection from Satan's power would be in context of transformation of shadow areas and complexes into a transcendent state beyond all opposites from a psychological/spiritual standpoint. The truth is what frees, even when it is rejected, and you along with it, by the world. What remains is a unity and what IS. The great I AM, in which all opposites are unified and transcended.

John 18:5-37 Whom are you looking for?...I am he...Whom are you searching for?...I told you I am he, and since I am the one you are after, let these others go...Put your sword away. Shall I not drink from the cup the Father has given me?...What I teach is widely known, for I have preached regularly in the synagogue and Temple; I have been heard by all the Jewish leaders and teach nothing in private that I have not said in public. Why are you asking me this question? Ask those who heard me. You have some of them here. They know what I said...If I lied, prove it. Should you hit a man for telling the truth?...'King' as you use the word or as the Jews use it?...I am not an earthly king. If I were, my followers would have fought when I was arrested by the Jewish leaders. But my Kingdom is not of the world...Yes, I was born for that purpose. And I came to bring truth to the world. All who love the truth are my followers.

Again we observe the final moments of Jesus' earthly life, but also John's continued emphasis on the importance of the truth and what matters not being confined to the relatively small realm of space/time.

John 19:11-30 You would have no power at all over me unless it were given to you from above. So those who brought me to you have the greater sin...He is your son...She is your mother!...I'm thirsty...It is finished.

It is indeed finished here on the cross. Jesus has fulfilled his purpose and individuation process!

John 20:15-29 Why are you crying? Whom are you looking for?... Mary!...don't touch me, for I haven't yet ascended to the Father. But go find my brothers and tell them that I ascend to my Father and your Father, my God and your God...As the Father has sent me, even so I am sending you....Receive the Holy Spirit. If you forgive anyone's sins, they are forgiven. If you refuse to forgive them, they are unforgiven...Put your finger into my hands. Put your hand into my side. Don't be faithless any longer. Believe!... You believe because you have seen me. But blessed are those who haven't seen me and believe anyway.

Jesus rises from the dead and says that his work now rests with us. Such is the nature of the Self; it requires life in the space-time frame for complete functionality. The Holy Spirit is our guide from the Christian perspective. We also have the famous Doubting Thomas episode here, and I have to admit it would be a great enhancer of faith to be shown God directly, which Jesus agrees to do here. Indeed, those who can believe without seeing are blessed, because humans are not intrinsically wired to have faith in this way. And conscious awareness, while necessary, is truly a gift and a curse, a cross unto itself.

John 21:3-22 Any fish, boys?...Throw out your net on the right-hand side of the boat, and you'll get plenty of them!...Bring some of the fish you've just caught...Now come and have some breakfast!...Simon, son of John, do you love me more than these others?...Then feed my lambs...Simon, son of John, do you really love me?...Then take care of my sheep...Simon, son of John, are you even my friend?...Then feed my little sheep. When you were young, you were able to do as you liked and go wherever you wanted to, but when you are old, you will stretch out your hands and others will direct you and take you where you don't want to go....Follow me...If I want him to live until I return, what is that to you? *You* follow me.

Jesus' instructions are to share what has been revealed and to take up the call to transformation both personally and for others' benefit in the same regard. This means the great symbol that is the cross, a true transformer between divine and human energies, must become our reality as well. It's very clear what the Self insists upon: YOU follow me.

## Conclusion and Direction

Jesus has illustrated some realities that are truly revolutionary, and we are currently experiencing another major evolution in God, as the era of the Holy Spirit is now in effect. The age of Pisces, that well-known symbol of Jesus, ended in 2000 A.D., and we are now in the Age of Aquarius. I'm not advocating for astrology here in any literal sense, but the meaning in certain cases like this cannot be ignored. We have seen that we must *unlearn what we have learned*, as Yoda reminds us in *Star Wars*. Each person must do this in his or her life for true transformation to occur. This is the hardest thing any of us will ever do. Just try and you'll know.

Gone are the days of saying we don't know anything about God's ways, especially as data in an argument for a point. Jesus has said that God is in each one of us and even revealed many things as noted in the Gospels. That excuse has been shown to be at least semi-untrue and also a burying of the God-given logical and consciousness capacities we have. Jesus said never to bury your talents. He also said to lean not on your own understanding. I'd listen to both statements here. Everything is a balance of faith and knowing God via experiences, which certain people in ever-increasing numbers do have, whether they know it or not. No one can know God fully, but there are things that are constantly revealed and observable. Also, no more believing what we want to believe or selectively picking views and angles in light of everything above. Following the herd like sheep accomplishes nothing by way of development and transformation as well. Let us not forget that *Jesus himself was labeled a blasphemer and a heretic*, and he turned out to be correct. Finally, true atheism has been discredited once and for all in this book.

A prescription for accomplishing these goals, arising from yet another culture with similar archetypal themes as Christianity, is the story of Black Elk of the Oglala Sioux Native American tribe. Notice how the effects of this psychological approach are nearly word for word what we have discussed and exactly what Jesus did:

> As a boy, when Black Elk was suffering from a severe illness and was almost in a coma, he had a tremendous vision or revelation in which he was transported to the skies where many horses came to him from the four points of the compass, where then he met the Grandfather Spirits and was given the healing plant for his people.

> Deeply shaken by his vision, the youth kept it to himself, as any normal human being would do, but later on he developed an acute phobia about thunderstorms, so that when even a little cloud appeared on the horizon, he would shake with fear.

> This forced him to consult a medicine man, who told him that he was ill because he had kept his vision to himself and had not shared it with his tribe. The medicine man said to Black Elk, "Nephew, I know now what the trouble is! You must do what the bay horse in your vision wanted you to do. You must perform this vision for your people upon earth. You must have the

horse-dance first for the people to see. Then the fear will leave you; but if you do not do this, something very bad will happen to you."

So Black Elk, who was then seventeen, and his father and mother and some other members of the tribe gathered together the exact number of horses--a certain number of white, a certain number of black, a certain number of sorrel, a certain number of buckskin, and one bay horse for Black Elk to ride.

Black Elk taught the songs that he had heard during his experience, and when the vision was enacted, it had a profound effect on the entire tribe, even a healing effect, with the result that the blind could see, the paralyzed walked, and other psychogenic diseases were cured[86].

The beginning of this tale reflects the state in which we find ourselves when we are overwhelmed by an encounter with the unconscious and the universal forces in our lives. We are traumatized and "shaken up" just like Black Elk was. Ultimately, the state of being "ill" reflects an insufficiently developed personality and an inability to respond properly. Something may happen in context of this, just like Black Elk experienced the vision in the sky, and we may feel that we cannot share what has happened to us.

The problem is that this defensive process of not facing the issue incurs psychological debt that eventually must be paid in some form. It leads to symptoms, and for Black Elk, he developed a

---

86.  M-L. Von Franz – The Interpretation of Fairy Tales (Rev. ed.), p. 31-32

phobia about *thunderstorms*, which not accidentally matches his traumatic experience in the *sky*.

Another example of this *symptoms matching problems* theme is an alcoholic "getting lost in the bottle" as the saying goes. With alcoholism, the problem often lies in *bottling up* feelings for one reason or another, and so the individual gets *literally lost in the bottle*.

We can also observe this process, for example, in obsessive-compulsive individuals who have contamination fears. Contamination involves a violation of one's borders (think immune system and how it identifies foreign invaders). Many people with obsessive-compulsive symptoms tend to have problems allowing psychological material into their lives for one reason or another, and so the symptom states the problem in symbolic form. The issue, in fact, *is* contamination, but *on another level*. The person actually needs to *allow* "contamination" by not guarding his or her borders so closely in context of those dynamics. Therefore, the symptom points the way to the cure in such cases.

This dynamic can also be potentially observed in the recent spikes in developmental disorders such as autism. People with these disorders have extreme difficulty in social interactions and often do not understand the social cues themselves. Our society has exploded technologically (smartphones, social networking sites, etc.) in recent years, and perhaps these developmentally-disabled individuals are a reminder to us that maybe we are forgetting how to interact with each other face-to-face. It isn't that one issue causes the other (the forces are not space-time bound), but rather that there is *meaning* to be found here. Synchronicity can manifest in this way as well. Remember, if something cannot be resolved (our personal distancing from each other) within, it is forced to appear externally, and in this case it may be the developmentally-disabled individuals who remind us of this problem.

Everything we have just discussed about symptoms matching problems and how these dynamics operate is consistent with the law of conservation or projection (nothing is created or destroyed, but rather shifts around and changes form). We need to learn to look at our problems in this way if we are going to have the proper conscious attitude to work through them. What we do not transform, we will transmit[87].

The psychological rule says that when an inner situation is not made conscious, it happens outside, as fate. That is to say, when the individual remains undivided and does not become conscious of his inner opposite, the world must perforce act out the conflict and be torn into opposing halves. (C.G. Jung)[88]

In comparison with Christ, the alchemical image is much the more complete as it contains a light and a dark side-the inferior part of human nature is included in it. (M-L Von Franz, noting what Jung said regarding the Philosopher's Stone)[89]

The opposites must be integrated and united. According to Dourley and many Jungians, the sun woman and her child in

---

87. see R. Rohr – CAC daily meditations
88. C.G. Jung – Aion  [CW 9(ii), para. 126, p. 71]
89. M-L Von Franz – Aurora Consurgens, p. 252

the Book of Revelation also join the opposites where the Mary-Jesus dynamic does not. In this and other areas, the seeds of further evolution are observed[90].

Returning to the story, Black Elk consults a medicine man (read: therapist, a helpful family member or friend, etc.) and begins to understand that he must face the reality of his vision. In other words, he has to become conscious in great detail (note the specific kinds of horses he is required to gather so he can perform his vision) of his psychological dynamics and then "confess" his experiences to others. This process of *confession* can be very healing because when people hold secrets that make them feel disconnected from others, it tends to have a self-poisoning effect.

The process of working through issues can be long and arduous, but the reward is great. When Black Elk was able to do so well enough to develop and transform, the change produced in him also caused profound changes in those around him. The language used in the tale is very similar to that attributed to the miracles of Jesus in the Christian New Testament as well.

This is exactly the process we have discussed regarding how self-development has an effect on others and the universe itself. And what is more, the key factor was the transformation in the person (Black Elk); the symptoms themselves were secondary and in service of the *person as a whole.*

We do not often see transformation without patience and time, but the willingness to hammer away at a problem until it cracks is also a key factor in healing. The phenomenon of the *quantum*

---

90.   see J. Dourley - On Behalf of the Mystical Fool: Jung on the Religious
      Situation

*leap* in the physical sciences illustrates this perfectly. Only when enough energy has been invested does an electron jump to the next energy level, and the same is true for us psychologically. Just because we do not see results doesn't mean nothing is happening. This is similar to the alchemical *circulatio*[91], where we must repeatedly face certain issues until they crack. Life is requiring us to put in a critical amount of energy, and only then will we be allowed to move to the next level of development and transformation. We have to go where we are afraid and dependent to accomplish this difficult task[92]. Our level of response-ability (!) is critical here[93].

> To develop one's own personality is indeed an unpopular undertaking, a deviation that is highly uncongenial to the herd, an eccentricity smelling of the cenobite, as it seems to the outsider. Small wonder, then, that from earliest times only the chosen few have embarked upon this strange adventure.... these personalities are as a rule the legendary heroes of mankind, the very ones who are looked up to, loved, and worshipped, the true sons of God whose names perish not.
>
> (C.G. Jung)[94]

Today, church is mostly within and in connection with others, not in an organized system or building. Each of us contains God within us, and the living connection must never be allowed to break. We

---

91. see M-L. Von Franz – Alchemy: An Introduction to the Symbolism and the Psychology
92. C.G. Jung – Dream Symbols of the Individuation Process.
93. from lecture given via the C.G. Jung Club of Orange County – The Cosmic Tree is Rending - by H. Fincher
94. C.G. Jung – The Development of Personality [CW 17, para. 298, p. 174]

are now witnessing a mass exodus from organized religions of all types, and this is not an accident. In fact, it is intended to keep the living connection alive via a warning about things not changing, provided people learn to assimilate the insights in this book and act on them. There is no correct spiritual system relative to others, just like no apostle was greater than the others. We have seen the same material in all of them, and Jesus sharply rebuked this type of arrogance with the apostles in that episode. More people have died in the name of organized religion (Crusades, Inquisition, bastardization of jihad, etc.) than any other entity.

And within each spiritual system, there is no more time for disputes over petty issues, such as whether or not Jesus is physically present in the Eucharist, etc. in the Christian tradition. It is the meaning, not the literal issue, that matters here. The same is true of the Resurrection; the meaning attached to it is more important than the event itself, and this actually enhances the value of what Jesus did. Events that occur at one period and are finished, failing to continue on, are effectively dead. Dying and rising is an ongoing process in each of us and all of nature. There can no longer be one-size-fits-all rituals from organized religion either. Finally, we have to stop evangelization. Let people be whatever faith they are, including spiritual but not religious. Your way is not likely to be someone else's way, and failure to introduce doubt into your way is a form of narcissistic arrogance. There is only one flag, as it were, and that flag is called God, no matter what image(s) (and there are many) one has for God.

What matters most to me is that the patient should reach his own view of things. Under my treatment a pagan becomes a pagan and a Christian a Christian, a Jew a Jew, according to what his destiny prescribes for him. (C.G. Jung)[95]

I am aware that Jesus said to preach the Gospel and God to all people, but he meant the gospel and God-image fitting *them*, not necessarily *you*. There is only one God anyway. God just incarnates in different ways and via different images, as noted above, and God is for everyone, as Jesus explicitly stated. Jung never committed to any religious system, and this was not an accident. Though he felt all systems had good things to offer, I think he knew that the goal was to be complete, as well as to *unite and transcend* all religious systems, just as is the goal with his four functions and the opposites themselves.

Another major problem that must be immediately squashed is the woke ideology that is far too prevalent today. This entire area is antithetical to any development or transformation, and it aims to destroy and rebuild in a way that completely violates nature, the universe, etc. This is also not up for debate and will lead us too far astray, but it must be noted as a non-political issue that people weaponize to do harm. You cannot cancel what you do not like, and if you do, eventually karma will find you via the unconscious taking matters into its own hands.

Nothing that doesn't evolve will survive in a meaningful way. Evolution occurs by moving in a circle-square-circle pattern. The initial circle is a state of *participation mystique*, or unconsciousness, like the Garden of Eden in the Judeo-Christian tradition. The square is the pointed realization of

---

95.   C.G. Jung – Memories, Dreams, Reflections, p. 138

reality in space-time, and the final circle is conscious awareness of reality at all levels[96]. This is the ultimate goal and the end or *opus* of the alchemical process.

> Woe betide those who live by way of examples! Life is not with
> them. If you live according to an example, you thus live the
> life of that example, but who should live your own life if not
> yourself? So live yourselves. (C.G. Jung)[97]

The Greek word *kenosis*, or emptying, for the purpose of doing just this, living *your* life, is critical to psychological development and living a complete life. That is the aim for which we must strive.

> And nature has no use for the plea that one "did not know."
> Not knowing acts like guilt.
>
> (C.G. Jung)[98]

This quote underscores the importance, yet again, of conscious awareness. It means everything. There is a 1995 video game called Chrono Trigger in which the hero, Crono, dies and must be restored to life. To accomplish this, the Time Egg, or Chrono Trigger, is required. It is said that it yields results equal to, "no more and no less," the energy the holder puts into the desired outcome. It is also said to be "pure potential." The egg in general is also an alchemical vessel of sorts[99]. There could be no better metaphor for what each of us is called to do regarding hatching our identities and ourselves (pun intended).

---

96.    see E.F. Edinger – The Mysterium Lectures
97.    from C.G. Jung – Liber Novus (The Red Book), p. 231
98.    C.G. Jung – The Development of Personality [CW 17, para. 91-92, p. 44]
99.    C.G. Jung – Dream Symbols of the Individuation Process

Conscious awareness is the key factor, and its implementation must be at the needed level and done by enough people to create meaningful development and transformation.

The gods and demons have not disappeared at all, they have merely got new names. They keep him on the run with restlessness, vague apprehensions, psychological complications, an invincible need for pills, alcohol, tobacco, dietary and other hygienic systems – and above, all, with an impressive array of neuroses. (C.G. Jung)[100]

Such problems are never solved by legislation or by tricks. They are solved only by a general change of attitude. And the change does not begin with propaganda and mass meetings, or with violence. It begins with a change in individuals. It will continue as a transformation of their personal likes and dislikes, of their outlook on life and of their values, and only the accumulation of these individual changes will produce a collective solution. (C.G. Jung)[101]

Everything now depends on man: immense power of destruction is given into his hand, and the question is whether he can resist the will to use it, and can temper his will with the spirit of love and wisdom. (C.G. Jung)[102]

---

100. from C.G. Jung – Symbols and the Interpretation of Dreams [CW 18, para. 555, pp. 241-242]

101. C.G. Jung – Psychology and Religion [CW 11, para. 135, p. 79]

102. from C.G. Jung – Answer to Job [CW 11, para. 745, p. 459]; also, Jung has noted that there is no guarantee that good or evil will prevail, though he believed we would have destroyed ourselves long ago had evil been the way of things. He felt that we would effectively squeak by with good barely winning out, provided we follow this quote.

We must pay attention to the above quotes. It is that serious. From the Christian perspective, each of us is a mixture of light and dark, good and evil, just like our Creator, and with the aid of the Holy Spirit today, we must bear this tension of opposites for the sake of development and transformation of ourselves and of God. And it is very difficult work, as Jesus notes in the non-canonical Gospel of Thomas:

Whoever is near me is near to the fire, and whoever is far from me is far from the Kingdom[103].

Identity, meaning, development, evolution, and transformation.

Being defeated by ever larger beings as we move along the spiral of individuation[104]. Not being perfect, but complete. The Navajo intentionally wove imperfections into their rugs and blankets to reflect this principle, as did Oriental cultures in things they made[105], which is reality.

This is our mandate. Go forth and connect yourself to God by the way you attempt this most difficult and important of tasks.

---

103. C.G. Jung – Dream Symbols of the Individuation Process (p. 189)
104. from a poem by Rainer Maria Rilke as cited in J. Hollis - A Life of Meaning
105. see H. Luke - Dark Wood to White Rose

## Appendix: DragonForce Songs

These are all highly psychological songs hitting on all our themes if you have ears to hear, especially the first three and the end of the fourth. The lyrics videos can be found on YouTube by typing the song followed by "lyrics video."

Through the Fire and Flames (2006 – Inhuman Rampage)

Ashes of the Dawn (2017 – Reaching Into Infinity)

Heroes of Our Time (2008 – Ultra Beatdown)

The Edge of the World (2017 – Reaching Into Infinity)

Valley of the Damned (2003 - Valley of the Damned)

The Last Journey Home (2008 – Ultra Beatdown)

War! (2017 – Reaching Into Infinity)

My Spirit Will Go On (2004 – Sonic Firestorm)

Seasons – (2012 - The Power Within)

Razorblade Meltdown (2019 – Extreme Power Metal)

Cry of the Brave (2004 – Sonic Firestorm)

Power and Glory (2014 – Maximum Overload)

Trail of Broken Hearts (2006 – Inhuman Rampage)

The Last Dragonborn (2019 - Extreme Power Metal)

The Game (2014 – Maximum Overload)

## About the Author

Joseph A. Talamo, Ph.D. (1981-), received his degree in clinical psychology with a specialization in depth psychology in 2009 from Pacifica Graduate Institute, his undergraduate degree from the University of Notre Dame in 2004, and attended Catholic schools from grades K, 2-6, and 10-12 as well as college. He has over 21 years of experience in clinical and academic settings and is the author of 2 articles (*Harry Potter and the Haunted Prophet; Archetypal Storm: Jung and the Music of DragonForce*), a book (*Black Storm: Development, Transformation, and Apocalyptic Moments*), and a dissertation (*A Jungian Depth Perspective on OCD*). Joseph enjoys sports (especially hockey, baseball, and football), fantasy sports, music (especially piano and DragonForce), chess, and occasionally resurrecting his video/computer game days. He is Pittsburgh, PA born and raised.

# References

Bly, R. (1990). *Iron John: A book about men.* New York: Vintage Books.

Bohm, D. (1980). *Wholeness and the implicate order.* New York: Routledge.

Campbell, J. (1968). *The hero with a thousand faces* (2nd ed.). Princeton, NJ: Princeton University Press.

Center for Action and Contemplation (CAC - Rohr, Richard). Daily Meditations (email – various years). Alburquerque, NM.

Corbett, L. (2022). *The God-image in Jung and the Monotheisms: A Study in Contrast.* Lecture delivered via the C.G. Jung Club of Orange County. Orange County, CA.

Dourley, J. (2010). *On behalf of the mystical fool: Jung on the religious situation.* New York: Routledge.

Edinger, E.F. (1984). *The creation of consciousness.* Toronto: Inner City Books.

Edinger, E.F. (1985). *Anatomy of the psyche.* Chicago: Open Court.

Edinger, E.F. (1986). *The Bible and the psyche: Individuation symbolism in the Old Testament.* Toronto: Inner City Books.

Edinger, E.F. (1992). *Ego and archetype.* Boston: Shambhala.

Edinger, E.F. (1994). *The eternal drama: The inner meaning of Greek mythology.* Boston: Shambhala.

Edinger, E.F. (1995). *Melville's Moby Dick: An American nekiya.* Toronto: Inner City Books.

Edinger, E.F. (1995). *The Mysterium lectures*. Toronto: Inner City Books.

Edinger, E.F. (1996). *The Aion lectures*. Toronto: Inner City Books.

Edinger, E.F. (1999). *Archetype of the apocalypse*. Chicago: Open Court.

Edinger, E.F. (1999). *The psyche in antiquity: Book two – Gnosticism and early Christianity*. Toronto: Inner City Books.

Edinger, E.F. (2000). *Ego and self: The Old Testament prophets*. Toronto: Inner City Books.

Edinger, E.F. (2002). *Science of the soul: A Jungian perspective*. Toronto: Inner City Books.

Fincher, H. (2023). *The Cosmic Tree is Rending*. Lecture delivered via the C.G. Jung Club of Orange County. Orange County, CA.

Hawking, S. & Mlodinow, L. (2010). *The Grand Design*. New York: Bantam Books.

Hollis, J. (1996). *Swamplands of the soul: New life in dismal places*. Toronto: Inner City Books.

Hollis, J. (2023). *A life of meaning: Relocating your center of spiritual gravity*. Boulder, CO: Sounds True.

Jung, C.G. (1966). Psychology and literature. In R.F.C. Hull (Trans.), *The collected works of C.G. Jung* (Vol. 15). Princeton, NJ: Princeton University Press. (Original work published 1950)

Jung, C.G. (1967). Symbols of transformation. In R.F.C. Hull (Trans.), *The collected works of C.G. Jung* (Vol. 5). Princeton, NJ: Princeton University Press. (Original work published 1912)

Jung, C.G. (1968). Archetypes of the collective unconscious. In R.F.C. Hull (Trans.), *The collected works of C.G. Jung* (Vol. 9(i)). Princeton, NJ: Princeton University Press. (Original work published 1954)

Jung, C.G. (1968). Psychology and alchemy. In R.F.C. Hull (Trans.), *The collected works of C.G. Jung* (Vol. 12). Princeton, NJ: Princeton University Press. (Original work published 1952)

Jung, C.G. (1969). Aion. In R.F.C. Hull (Trans.), *The collected works of C.G. Jung* (Vol. 9(ii)). Princeton, NJ: Princeton University Press. (Original work published 1951)

Jung, C.G. (1969). Answer to Job. In R.F.C. Hull (Trans.), *The collected works of C.G. Jung* (Vol. 11). Princeton, NJ: Princeton University Press. (Original work published 1952)

Jung, C.G. (1969). Psychology and religion. In R.F.C. Hull (Trans.), *The collected works of C.G. Jung* (Vol. 11). Princeton, NJ: Princeton University Press. (Original work published 1938)

Jung, C.G. (1969). Synchronicity: An acausal connecting principle. In R.F.C. Hull (Trans.), *The collected works of C.G. Jung* (Vol. 8). Princeton, NJ: Princeton University Press. (Original work published 1952)

Jung, C.G. (1970). Mysterium coniunctionis. In R.F.C. Hull (Trans.), *The collected works of C.G. Jung* (Vol. 14). Princeton, NJ: Princeton University Press. (Original work published 1955/1956)

Jung, C.G. (1970). The state of psychotherapy today. In R.F.C. Hull (Trans.), *The collected works of C.G. Jung* (Vol. 10).

Princeton, NJ: Princeton University Press. (Original work published 1934)

Jung, C. G. (1971). Psychological types. In H. G. Baynes (Trans.), *The collected works of C.G. Jung* (Vol. 6). Princeton, NJ: Princeton University Press. (Original work published 1921)

Jung, C.G. (1976). Symbols and the interpretation of dreams. In R.F.C. Hull (Trans.), *The collected works of C. G. Jung* (Vol. 18). Princeton, NJ: Princeton University Press. (Original work published 1961)

Jung, C.G. (1989). *Memories, dreams, reflections.* New York: Vintage Books. (Original work published 1963)

Jung, C.G. (2009). *Liber novus.* New York: W.W. Norton

Jung, C.G. (2019). *Dream symbols of the individuation process: Notes of the seminar given on Wolfgang Pauli's dreams.* Suzanne Geiser (ed.). Philemon Series. Princeton University Press, Princeton, NJ.

Jung, C.G. (2022). *Consciousness and the unconscious: Lectures delivered at ETH Zurich, Vol. 2 (1934).* Ernst Falzeder (ed.). Philemon Series. Princeton University Press: Princeton, NJ.

Jung, C.G. (2023). *Jung on Ignatius of Loyola's Spiritual Exercises: Lectures delivered at ETH Zurich, Vol. 7 (1939-1940).* Martin Liebscher (ed.) Philemon Series. Princeton University Press: Princeton, NJ.

Jung, E. & Von Franz, M-L. (1998). *The Grail Legend* (2nd ed.). Princeton, NJ: Princeton University Press. (Original work published 1960)

Luke, H. (1989). *Dark wood to white rose: Journey and transformation in Dante's Divine Comedy.* Morning Light Press. Original Work published 1975.

Kalsched, D. (1996). *The inner world of trauma.* New York: Brunner-Routledge.

Kalsched, D. (2013). *Trauma and the soul.* New York: Routledge.

LeGuin, U. (1971). *The Tombs of Atuan.* New York: Simon Pulse.

Levine, P. (1997). *Waking the Tiger: Healing trauma.* Berkeley, CA: North Atlantic Books

Main, R. (1997). *Encountering Jung: Jung on synchronicity and the paranormal.* Princeton, NJ: Princeton University Press.

Rowling, J.K. (1997). *Harry Potter and the Sorcerer's Stone.* New York: Scholastic.

Rowling, J.K. (1999). *Harry Potter and the Chamber of Secrets.* New York: Scholastic.

Rowling, J.K. (1999). *Harry Potter and the Prisoner of Azkaban*: New York: Scholastic.

Rowling, J.K. (2000). *Harry Potter and the Goblet of Fire.* New York: Scholastic.

Rowling, J.K. (2003). *Harry Potter and the Order of the Phoenix*: New York: Scholastic.

Rowling, J.K. (2005). *Harry Potter and the Half-Blood Prince.* New York: Scholastic.

Rowling, J.K. (2007). *Harry Potter and the Deathly Hallows.* New York: Scholastic.

Schwartz-Salant, N. (1982). Narcissism and character *transformation: The psychology of narcissistic character disorders.* Toronto: Inner City Books.

Talamo, J. (2010). *M Theory and the Cosmic Self.* Unpublished manuscript.

Ulanov, A. (2001). *Finding space: Winnicott, God, and psychic reality.* Westminster John Knox Press, Louisville, KY.

Von Franz, M-L. (1980). *Alchemy: An introduction to the symbolism and the psychology.* Toronto: Inner City Books.

Von Franz, M-L. (1993). *Psychotherapy.* Boston: Shambhala. (Original work published 1990)

Von Franz, M-L. (1996). *The interpretation of fairy tales* (Rev. ed.). Boston: Shambhala.

Von Franz, M-L. (1998). *C.G. Jung: His myth in our time.* Toronto: Inner City Books. (Original work published 1972)

Von Franz, M-L. (2000). *Aurora Consurgens.* Toronto: Inner City Books. (Original work published 1966)

Woodman, M. (1982). *Addiction to perfection.* Toronto: Inner City Books.

Made in the USA
Las Vegas, NV
05 December 2023

82122605R00128